The Teller in the Tale

THE *Teller* IN THE TALE ✍ by

Louis D. Rubin, Jr.

UNIVERSITY OF WASHINGTON PRESS

Seattle and London

Copyright © 1967 by the University of Washington
Press

Library of Congress Catalog Card Number 67–21197
Manufactured by the Colonial Press Inc., Clinton, Mass.

Printed in the United States of America

To C. Hugh Holman

Preface

THIS book is an attempt, on a small scale, to put the novelist back into the novel. Not that he has ever been out of the novel, of course, or that most people who read novels do not know that he *is* in it. One might well reply, "but of course, all that goes without saying." Yet much criticism of fiction, and much theorizing about the nature of fiction, is written almost as if the novelist were not supposed to be present—as if novels were objective dramatizations written by authors who, if they knew what they were about, were careful never to let the reader suspect that they were telling him a story. "Don't tell it; show it," the catchphrase goes. And any consideration of the novelist has been handled as if biographical, not literary, interests were involved.

It has always seemed to me that to talk about a novel without talking about the author is to omit a very important aspect of one's experience, and delight, in reading novels: the personality of the novelist. The novelist *belongs* in the novel; and pretending that he isn't there, I feel, is foolish business. But how *is* he there? I hold with the general notion that there is a distinct difference between literary criticism and biographical inquiry, and that a novel, like a poem or a play, is a work of art and is to be judged in terms of its formal dimensions. I believe, that is, in the principles of formalist criticism. Anything else is not criticism, but historical or biographical inquiry.

Several years ago I read two books which, once I had absorbed them, seemed to point to an answer. The first of these was Henry Nash Smith's brilliant study, *Mark Twain: The Development of a Writer.* In the course of this book Smith showed the process whereby Twain created a narrative persona to tell his stories, most notably in *The Adventures of Huckleberry Finn.* The other book was Wayne Booth's *The Rhetoric of Fiction.* It took a while for the full implications of this remarkable book to become clear to me. Booth took the position that all novels are works of rhetoric, and that the reader, in reading the novel, necessarily accepted the rhetorical relationship between novelist and reader—knew, in short, that he was being told a story, not being given a counterfeit demonstration of real life, and that the way the novelist told him the story was essential to the way he responded to it. Especially in his discussion of the implied author of a novel was Booth illuminating, for he expressed, what I had always felt about novels but had never been able to verbalize: that a novel is told by an implied author, who is created by the biographical author and is part of the formal experience of the novel.

In a very real sense, the book that follows constitutes an exploration of certain aspects of Wayne Booth's book. If I cite *The Rhetoric of Fiction* but seldom, that is because its impress really appears on almost every page. I decided to reread some of my favorite novels, and to pay special attention to the way in which the implied author, the authorial personality telling the story, figures in the meaning of the book. What does he do? What role does he play? To what extent does one's experience in reading the novel actively involve the presence of the novelist?

In the chapters that follow, I have sought to discuss Stendhal, Mark Twain, Henry James, Marcel Proust, James Joyce, and François Mauriac, and a few other novelists in passing, with this consideration in mind. Not, however, with *only* this consideration in mind; my critical "method"—if I may dignify my way of reading novels by calling it by any such name—is all too impure and too little conceptualistic by nature to enable me to confront novels so singlemindedly. Much of what I have to say, of course, has long since been said, and said better; these chapter-length discussions of writers and their works, using translations for the French novelists, can obviously add little to the extensive body of scholarship that now exists on each of them. If I have anything to contribute beyond the testimony of my own delight in these writers and their books, it probably lies not so much in any originality of idea or insight, as in the emphasis I give to the workings of the authorial personality, an emphasis which I think has not generally been given. I hope that in so doing I can encourage a more widespread recognition of this particular aspect of novel reading in order that critics wiser and more discriminating than I may use it in writing about, and thinking about, prose fiction.

The writing of this book was made possible through the generosity of three fine institutions. I am grateful to Hollins College, Virginia, and in particular to President John A. Logan, Jr., for granting me a year's leave of absence from my teaching duties in order to undertake it; to the American Council of Learned Societies, and in particular to Mr. Charles Blitzer, its executive associate, for awarding me a fellowship to pursue the project; and to the University of North Carolina, and in particular to C. Hugh Holman and George M. Harper, for inviting me to offer a graduate seminar in the subject of this book while I was writing it. My term's stay at Chapel Hill, under the auspices of the Cooperative Program in the Humanities of the University of North Carolina and Duke University, made it possible for me to expose my ideas on the topic to the tender mercies of some excellent graduate students and others, to my own immeasurable benefit—so much so, in fact, that I have recently joined the staff of that institution. But had it not been for the interest and the keen intellectual stimulation that came of teaching the fine undergraduate English students of Hollins College over a ten-year period, I am sure that I should never have reached the point at which this book began to take shape in my mind.

Among many to whom my debt is great throughout this several-year process, and whose help I should like especially to acknowledge, are: Julia Randall Sawyer, Richard H. W. Dillard, and all of the English faculty at Hollins College; Howard Nemerov, of the faculty of Brandeis University and in 1962–1963 writer-in-residence at Hollins College; C. Carroll Hollis, of the University of North Carolina; John W. Aldridge, of the University of Michigan and formerly visiting professor at Hollins College; Robert D. Jacobs, of the University of Kentucky; and Robert M. Figg, III, of the University of South Florida and formerly of Hollins College.

I am grateful to *The Kenyon Review*, Gambier, Ohio, and to *The Southern Review*, Baton Rouge, Louisiana, for permission to reprint the chapters entitled "The Self Recaptured" and "François Mauriac, or, the Novelist as Theologian," respectively, both of which appeared in somewhat different form in those periodicals.

Louis D. Rubin, Jr.

Chapel Hill, North Carolina

Contents

The Teller in the Tale

ONE · Concerning Cide Hamete Benengeli and Others

EARLY in the second book of *Don Quixote,* Sancho Panza arrives at the house of his master with some news which he is sure will be of the greatest interest to the still convalescent Knight of the Woeful Countenance. It seems that the adventures in which they had recently been engaged have been made into a book. Sancho has learned this from Sampson, son of their fellow townsman Bartholomew Carrasco, who had been away at Salamanca studying for his bachelor's degree. "When I went to welcome him home," Sancho informs Quixote, "he told me that your worship's story is already in print under the title of *The Ingenious Don Quixote de la Mancha.* He says that I'm mentioned too under my own name of Sancho Panza, and so is the lady Dulcinea del Toboso, and so are other matters which happened to us in private." [1] Sancho finds this all very astounding; how, he wonders, could the story writer have learned this?

Quixote himself has no doubts. You may be sure, he tells Sancho, that the author must be "some sage enchanter." But how can that be, Sancho objects, when apparently the author's name is known—is he not one Cide Hamete Aubergine, which as they both agree is a Moorish name? To clear up the mystery, Sancho goes to bring Sampson Carrasco to see his master. That worthy informs Quixote that the author's name is Cide Hamete

---

1. Miguel de Cervantes, *Don Quixote, trans.* J. M. Cohen, Penguin Classics ed. (Harmondsworth, Middlesex, England, 1950), p. 484.

Benengeli—not Aubergine as Sancho had erroneously reported —and that thanks to this Moor and to his translator, Quixote is now one of the most famous knights errant ever to appear "on all the rotundity of the earth." More than 12,000 copies of his adventures have already been printed in Portugal, Barcelona, and Valencia, and an edition is rumored to be in preparation at Antwerp.[2]

The conversation continues for several days, and at one point Quixote asks a question. Does the author promise a second book of adventures? Sampson Carrasco is not sure. "Yes, he does, but he says he has not found it and does not know who has it. And so we are in doubt whether it will come out or not."[3] Thereupon they discuss the economics of writing and publishing, and after that it is not long before Don Quixote and Sancho Panza begin making plans for a new foray into knight errantry.

Whether or not Miguel de Cervantes was the first true novelist—certainly he was the first good one—he was one of the very earliest practitioners of what has especially in the last hundred years become the predominant literary form. Prose fiction as we know it today more or less began with Cervantes. Because of this, one excuses his awkwardnesses, his often primitive technique, on the ground that he wrote before the form had evolved into its present state. He did not realize, as we now do, that the object of the novelist, as Ford Madox Ford wrote of Joseph Conrad, "is to keep the reader entirely oblivious of the fact that the author exists—even of the fact that he is reading a book."[4] A passage such as that quoted above, in which Cervantes has a fine time pretending that his book was written

2. *Ibid.*, p. 486.
3. *Ibid.*, p. 494.
4. Quoted in Miriam Allott, *Novelists on the Novel* (New York and London, 1959), p. 273.

by someone else and letting his characters talk about themselves as if they were real people, is obviously no way to keep the reader oblivious of the author's existence, or to make him forget that it is only a book he is reading; quite the contrary. And thus Cervantes surely laid himself open to strictures similar to those passed by Henry James on Anthony Trollope, to the effect that

he concedes to the reader that he and his trusting friend are only "making believe." He admits that the events he narrates have not really happened, and that he can give his narrative any turn the reader may like best. Such a betrayal of a sacred office seems to me, I confess, a terrible crime. . . . It implies that the novelist is less occupied in looking for the truth than the historian, and in so doing it deprives him at a stroke of all his standing-room.[5]

Perhaps. James's comment—which, I hasten to add, differs from James's *practice* as a novelist himself—represents a fairly widespread assumption of what fiction is and how it works. Even so, it might be well to consider just what is taking place in that passage from Book II of *Don Quixote,* and what this might possibly tell us about the art of fiction.

We are, to be sure, conscious of the author's presence when we read it. We do not miss the irony of the characters talking about whether there is to be a second book of adventures, when what we are reading is that second book. If we know much about Cervantes we doubtless realize, too, that the episode is a stab at the false author who produced a counterfeit sequel to Book I shortly after it was published. But does it follow that in being thus reminded by the author that what we are reading is make believe, we lose any kind of belief in truth? On the contrary, the passage, coming when it does, has the effect of making

5. Henry James, "The Art of Fiction," in *The Future of the Novel,* ed. Leon Edel, Vintage ed. (New York, 1956), p. 6.

Sancho Panza, Quixote, and Sampson Carrasco seem if anything more, rather than less, real. For especially in their commenting on Cide Hamete Benengeli's history of their adventures, they seem very believable folk.

What Cervantes is actually doing there, I think, is intensifying, not destroying, the so-called illusion of reality that fiction is supposed to provide. Having put his characters through a series of fictional adventures, he now makes them talk about the book they have just taken part in, which adds to their credibility by making them seem more lifelike, and less artificial, than ever: He does this *at the same time* as he reminds us that we have been told and are at that moment being told a story. He even jokes about it with us; when Sampson Carrasco tells Quixote that some readers "would have been glad if the authors had left out a few of the countless beatings which Don Quixote received in various encounters," Sancho remarks that "that's where the truth of the story comes in" ! [6] Truth of the story? But none of it is true; it is all fiction, all make believe. Of course: But it *seems* like the truth, it seems real, and never more so than at such moments—moments when, to repeat, we are quite aware of the author's presence and forcefully reminded that we are, in utter violation of Ford Madox Ford's dictum, reading a novel.

The explanation of this apparent paradox, I think, lies in the nature of the curious transaction between novel, novelist, and reader that is known as storytelling, and that is supposed to produce an illusion of reality whereby the reader, though well aware that the people described in a novel are fictional and that the events described in the novel never actually took place, becomes convinced that he is observing real life. Whether called myth,

6. *Don Quixote*, p. 488.

fable, romance, fiction, or whatever, the art of storytelling consists of persuading the reader willingly to suspend his disbelief
in the reality of the story being recounted, and thereupon re-
warding him by giving him a representation of reality that furnishes order and meaning to the experience described—something
which real life often fails to provide. In *War and Peace*, Pierre
Bezukhov acts out the drama of human engagement in time
and society in such a way that, by involving ourselves with him
and taking his situation seriously, we gain a sense of what his
engagement means. We thus acquire knowledge, both in the
sense that our perception of the meaning of Bezukhov's experience tells us something about the meaning of all human
experience including our own, and also that by sharing Bezukhov's activity we come to understand how it feels to be undergoing that experience. Whether this is measurable, verifiable,
or even useful knowledge is something else again; apparently
Plato did not think so. Even if it is all no more than a pleasant
amusement (which I do not myself concede for a minute),
people do read novels (and see plays, and listen to string quar-
tets, and so on) for approximately these reasons.

Apparently everything depends on the illusion of reality.
Without it, the novel will mean nothing, the play will fail to
come across. If we attend the local amateur theater group's
production of *Macbeth*, with our next-door neighbor's wife
playing the role of Lady Macbeth, unless we can be made to
believe that it is the wife of a tenth-century Scottish lord
clutching a dagger on the stage, we are unlikely to consider
that Duncan is in any danger. But such is Shakespeare's genius
that with only a modicum of talent on the part of the actress
we are soon plunged into the dramatic illusion, and we become
much more interested in what will happen to Duncan and to
Macbeth than in how well our neighbor's wife is performing.

Similarly, we know quite well that Don Quixote and Sancho Panza are fictional characters created by Miguel de Cervantes, and that they never actually walked the historical soil of Spain, but Cervantes' skill is so persuasive that we soon forget that fact, and when the Knight of the Woeful Countenance decides that the windmills are really giants in disguise and sets out to engage them in unequal combat, we fear for his continued good health, and sympathize deeply with poor Sancho in his unsuccessful attempt to make his employer see what he is about to do.

This is the illusion of reality, the willing suspension of disbelief. But does either our neighbor's wife's portrayal of Lady Macbeth, or Cervantes' fictional characters' roles as Quixote and Sancho, ever make us think that we are, after all, witnessing real life instead of art? No, indeed. We do not for a minute really fear that a man sleeping in a room directly offstage is about to be murdered; if we did, we would shout for the police. And similarly, Don Quixote may have thought that Amadis of Gaul was an actual historical figure, but we know that Don Quixote wasn't and isn't. If we thought he was, we should very likely put down the book in disgust; for Cervantes to be jocular about a poor deluded madman would seem a serious breach of good taste.

In other words, if a novel is to succeed in interesting us it is essential not only that there be created the illusion of reality, but that we remain quite aware that it *is* an illusion. In Aristotelian terms, the action must not only be "probable" but also "impossible." We must *know* that it is only a story, and nothing more or less than that. Just as, with the amateur production of *Macbeth*, we will suspend our disbelief and pretend that our next-door neighbor's wife is about to murder a sleeping guest only if the initiative and the option to do so lie with us; it must be a willing suspension, which we can offer to do or not as we see fit.

In short, no matter how intense the dramatic illusion, no matter how gripping the plot or believable the characterization, if we are to enter imaginatively into a work of fiction we must at all times feel that it is fiction, that a story is being told to us. The two parts of the equation—that it be *like* real life, and it *not be* real life—are absolutely indispensable.

To return to Cide Hamete Benengeli, the apparent intrusion of the author into the story by reminding us that we are dealing with make believe does not shatter our illusion of reality, but only serves to reinforce, by pointing out the paradox involved, our sense of the existence of this artistic relationship between author and character, between art and real life. We *know* the story is being told to us, and this no matter how vivid the author's skill at portraiture, or how firm his grasp of the details of a scene. The illusion is always there, and so is the awareness that it is an illusion. By slyly reminding us of its existence, as Cervantes does, the author can intensify our conscious delight in our participation in the artistic process, and can also push it one step further by making his characters seem momentarily to be taking part in the illusion along with us. At such a time, without losing for a minute their authority as characters, they seem to become even more lifelike (and more illusory) than ever.

We know that when we are reading a novel we are being told a story, and we know that an author is telling the story to us. Yet we seem quickly to lose sight of this when we begin theorizing about how novels function. Any development, any authorial intrusion, which reminds us that we are embarked upon a pretense of reality, we declare to be a sin against the truth of fiction. The novelist's objective, we say, is to enable us to pretend that we are reading real life, and in real life there is no author to explain every happening. The author must so efface himself, so disguise his presence, that we can forget he is there. Yet we never for a minute forget it. The author need not, as Fielding does, deliver philosophical essays, or like George Eliot, lecture us on what is going on inside his characters' minds, for us to be able to sense his presence. We know he is there by his tone, by the language he uses, by the things he says are important, by the kinds of insights with which he provides us all along the way. Is any novelist, for example, more ceaselessly and magnificently present at all times during his narration than Joseph Conrad?

Captain MacWhirr wiped his eyes. The sea that had nearly taken him overboard had, to his great annoyance, washed his sou'-wester hat off his bald head. The fluffy, fair hair, soaked and darkened, resembled a mean skein of cotton threads festooned round his bald skull. His face, glistening with sea-water, had been made crimson with the wind, with the sting of sprays. He looked as though he had come off sweating from before a furnace.[7]

This is not real life, but an artist describing real life, and no matter how immersed we become in the story of Captain Mac-Whirr and his confrontation with the typhoon—"Typhoon" is one of the greatest sea stories ever written—we never lose our appreciation of Conrad's skill at telling the story. In other stories Conrad has his man Marlow relate what happens; no matter, we still retain, as an essential and irreplaceable part of our experience of reading the story, the awareness of the author putting words into Marlow's mouth.

Authorial intrusion is something of a dirty word nowadays. And of course, expressed that way, it has to be. An intruder is

7. Joseph Conrad, "Typhoon," in *Typhoon and Other Stories* (New York, 1928), p. 64.

somebody who forces his presence into somewhere he does not not belong. Unfortunately, however, the term has come to mean, in much critical practice, the very assertion of the author's presence. But the author's presence in his narrative is not necessarily an intrusion into it; that is, he isn't always where he does not belong. When, for example, Henry James tells us in *The Ambassadors* what Lambert Strether's feelings are upon discovering, in the course of a walk in the countryside, Chad Newsome and Mme. de Vionnet out boating together, he remarks:

Why indeed—apart from oddity—the situation should have been really stiff, was a question naturally not practical at the moment, and in fact, so far as we are concerned, a question tackled, later on and in private, only by Strether himself. He was to reflect later on and in private that it was mainly *he* who had explained—as he had had moreover comparatively little difficulty in doing.[8]

Strether doesn't violate that chronology; James does, and he tells it to us—*we*, author to reader—because he feels that even though Strether at the moment of the confrontation had no time to analyze his feelings, we ought to know then what he later decided about them. Certainly we do not object to having this bit of information given us, even though it comes from the author and not from Strether. James's presence as author isn't an unwanted intrusion, but a welcome aid to our participation in his story.

The author's presence becomes not an aid but an intrusion only when, instead of helping us to take part in a fictional situation, it impedes us from doing so. In Ellen Glasgow's novel *Barren Ground*, for example, the heroine, Dorinda Oakley, is jilted by her artistocratic swain, and departs from rural Vir-

8. Henry James, *The Ambassadors*, ed. S. P. Rosenbaum, Norton Critical ed. (New York, 1964), p. 309.

ginia for New York, where she begins hunting for a job. To wit:

All day she walked from one stony street to another, stopping to rest now and then on a bench in one of the squares, where she would sit motionless for hours, watching the sparrows. Her food, usually a tough roll and a sausage of dubious tenderness, she bought at the cheapest place she could find and carried, wrapped in newspaper, to the bench where she rested. Her only hope, she felt, lay in the dogged instinct which told her that when things got as bad as they could, they were obliged, if they changed at all, to change for the better. There was no self-pity in her thoughts. The unflinching Presbyterian in her blood steeled her against sentimentality. She would meet life standing and she would meet it with her eyes open; but she knew that the old buoyant courage, the flowing outward of the spirit, was over for ever.[9]

Obviously the author, not Dorinda Oakley, is informing us that there was "no self-pity in her thoughts" and that "the unflinching Presbyterian in her blood steeled her against sentimentality." But does the author know what she is talking about? Not if the final sentence of the paragraph is an accurate representation of what Dorinda Oakley is thinking, because for the young woman to sit down there on the park bench and tell herself that she is going to "meet life standing" and "with her eyes open," and also to think about herself as having had "the old buoyant courage, the outward flowing of the spirit," which is now "over for ever," is to melodramatize herself quite romantically, and also to display more than a little inconsistency. When the author, therefore, tells us that Dorinda is one thing, and shows us Dorinda as quite another thing, then she obviously cannot always recognize self pity and sentimentality. The author is being sentimental about Dorinda Oakley, and we feel that her attempt

9. Ellen Glasgow, *Barren Ground* (New York, 1925), p. 198.

to tell us that Dorinda isn't what she manifestly is, indeed constitutes an intrusion.

It is an intrusion because it cripples the authority, not of what is being told us, but of the novelist who is telling it to us. The passage tells us that the novelist doesn't know what she is talking about, that she cannot be trusted to interpret the meaning of the events she is describing. This is a very different matter from Anthony Trollope, or Cervantes, reminding us that the story we are reading did not really happen, and is only make believe. We know that already, and the knowledge does not cause us any concern. In this instance, rather, the author is being revealed as an imperfect interpreter of her own story, when in order for the story to mean what the author insists it means, we have got to trust her pronouncements.

"Authorial intrusion," then, is not a matter of the reader's sensing the presence of the author telling the story and commenting to us about what it means, but of the reader's being told things by the author which are obviously inconsistent. The author is wrenching the facts into place in order to make a point, and it is obvious to us that those facts—the characterization, the plot—do not belong in that shape and do not add up to that point. When Conrad tells us that Captain MacWhirr, almost drowned by a massive wave, is annoyed because he has lost his hat, we believe him; that is obviously the kind of person Captain MacWhirr is. When Ellen Glasgow tells us that Dorinda Oakley is not sentimental and is without self pity, and then shows her thinking to herself that "she would meet life standing and she would meet it with her eyes open; but she knew that the old buoyant courage, the flowing outward of the spirit, was over for ever," we do not quite believe her.

If the principle is understood that it is not the narrative's fidelity to truth as such that the reader of a novel must be made to accept, but rather the storyteller's fidelity to the story, a great deal of confusion about authorial authority, verisimilitude, illusion of reality and so forth can be cleared up. The reader of a novel understands and insists that he is reading fiction, that it is make believe, and he does not need to be tricked into forgetting this. He does demand, however, that granted the essential make believe involved in fiction, which is to say, granted that he is being told a story and is not being exposed to real life, the author's relation to his story, the way in which he presents it to us, must seem *artistically* truthful, *artistically* appropriate. When we read a ghost story, for example, it matters not a bit that we do not really believe in the existence of ghosts. We are quite willing to enter into the make believe involved in the story; we accept the artistic convention, which is, Let us pretend with the author that there is such a thing as a supernatural spirit surviving after death and continuing to concern itself with life. But what the author tells us about the ghost, and what he makes the ghost do, had better coincide with our notions of appropriate behavior under the circumstances, or we will put the book down for good. Not the truth of the subject, but the truth of the artistry, must convince us. And the artistry involves the consciousness of the presence of an artist. When that artist, if she is named Ellen Glasgow, informs us that Dorinda Oakley sits on a park bench in New York for hours watching sparrows, we accept the statement. But when she tells us that Dorinda is unsentimental and without self pity, and at the same time what she tells us Dorinda is thinking seems sentimental and self pitying, we withdraw our assent, no longer suspend our disbelief, and so on. The author intrudes, we declare. We mean by this, not simply that the author is present, but more importantly, that she is being inconsistent.

"We take for granted by the general law of fiction a primary author," Henry James says in writing about Joseph Conrad; but then he adds at once that we "Take him so much for granted that we forget him in proportion as he works upon us, and that he works upon us most in fact by making us forget him." [10] Do we indeed? The truth of this statement depends on what is meant by "forget." When Strether comes upon Chad Newsome and Mme. de Vionnet in the countryside, and James tells us what Strether would later on think of the moment of confrontation, are we jolted into a consciousness of artifice because James has for the moment violated his convention of not directly addressing the reader himself? Not in the least. We have all along taken James's presence for granted. To take something for granted is not to forget its existence, then; if it were, we should have been quite disconcerted when James broke in to tell us what he did. Rather, by taking the author's presence for granted, we mean only that we cease consciously to think about him all the time. This is a very different matter from forgetting he is there; quite the reverse, in fact.

Again, when expressed in this way this all seems quite obvious. But too often a critic writing about the novel seems to proceed without keeping in mind the elementary fact that fiction is told to us by a novelist, not presented anonymously for our inspection. James's remark about taking the novelist's presence for granted has been built into a rigid dictum—of which Ford Madox Ford's assertion about the need for keeping the reader oblivious of the fact that he is reading a book is an example— which says that the novelist blunders to the extent that he reveals his own presence in telling his story. Jean Paul Sartre's attack on

10. Henry James, "The New Novel," in *The Future of the Novel*, p. 281.

François Mauriac for playing God in his fiction is a classic example of this position:

> there is no more place for a privileged observer in a real novel than in the world of Einstein. . . . M. Mauriac has . . . chosen divine omniscience and omnipotence. But novels are written *by* men and *for* men. In the eyes of God, Who cuts through appearance and goes beyond them, there is no novel, there is no art, for art thrives on appearances. God is not an artist. Neither is M. Mauriac.[11]

Sartre's position here is an exaggerated manifestation of much modern critical rigidity concerning the necessity for the so-called effaced author. But while the novel Sartre is criticizing, Mauriac's *The End of the Night*, is almost as bad as Sartre says it is, this not because the author is present when he should remain effaced, paring his fingernails like Stephen Dedalus' invisible artist. The essence of Mauriac's art is bound up in the conflict between his Jansenism and his sensualism; and much of the excitement of the fiction lies in the reader's awareness of Mauriac fighting the matter out within himself as he writes. In Mauriac's lesser work, of which *The End of the Night* is an example, this conflict is largely missing, not because Mauriac intrudes his own personality into the plight of his people, but because, paradoxically, he fails to do so. He withdraws from his role as novelist, which requires an emotional involvement in his people as human beings like himself, and takes to the pulpit to preach, with his characters being forced to become bodiless figures of religious allegory in order that he may demonstrate his theology. It is not a question of whether Mauriac's personality should or should not be present in his novels; rather, it is a matter of *how* that personality is present.

11. Jean Paul Sartre, "François Mauriac and Freedom," in *Literary and Philosophical Essays*, trans. Annette Michelson (New York, 1955), p. 23.

A novelist's presence can make itself felt in more than one way, and the artistic success of a novel will depend on how this is accomplished. I have already sought to show instances in which both Henry James and Ellen Glasgow intrude their presences into their narrative, and have suggested that where James gives us valuable information, Miss Glasgow tries to tell us something about her heroine that does not seem valid. The difference is not intrusion, but validity. And the measurement of that validity is indeed one of truth—of artistic truth, of whether or not what is told and shown is appropriate to the artistic situation. To see what is involved here, let us briefly consider two crucial incidents in what has often been called the greatest of all American novels, *The Adventures of Huckleberry Finn*.

When Huck Finn learns that his companion Jim has been sold by the Duke and the Dauphin, and is imprisoned on Phelps Farm, he tries to decide whether to go rescue him. His conscience tells him that it is sinful and wicked to help a Negro slave escape from captivity, but at the same time his friendship for Jim makes him want to set him free. The friendship wins out over the socially imposed restraints of conscience, and Huck leaves for Phelps Farm. This is a great scene, and when Huck says to himself, "all right then, I'll *go* to Hell," it is one of the triumphant moments in all of American literature.[12]

When Huck gets to Phelps Farm, however, he is unsure how to go about the job, but as he begins talking with the farmer's wife, it suddenly turns out that she thinks he is Huck's friend Tom Sawyer, come all the way down from Missouri to Arkansas to pay a visit to his aunt and uncle: "it was like being born again, I was so glad to find out who I was," Huck tells us.[13]

---

12. Mark Twain, *The Adventures of Huckleberry Finn*, intro. by Lionel Trilling, Rinehart ed. (New York, 1948), p. 214.
13. *Ibid.*, p. 224.

This scene, built on an almost unbelievable coincidence, is anything but a triumph, if most commentaries on the novel are to be believed: and the whole sequence of Jim's rescue that follows, with Tom masquerading as his brother Sid and Huck as Tom, is of disputed artistic merit.

What is the difference between the success of the first scene as fiction, and the failure of the second? In neither is the novelist actually present, if by present is meant that a novelist is directly addressing us without regard to the fictional action. Mark Twain is thoroughly effaced throughout the narrative, which is told by Huck and in Huck's own language. Nevertheless, the author is quite active and in our consciousness in both scenes. We object to the sudden, gratuitous turning-up of Tom Sawyer, and Huck's arrival at the one plantation in all of Arkansas where Tom is momentarily expected, on the quite proper ground that esthetic probability is rudely violated. This happens, we say, because the author needs to end his book, and he wants to bring Tom Sawyer back into the story for that purpose. We simply do not believe that it happened; we see all too clearly that Mark Twain has wrenched his whole plot structure out of shape in order to get Tom back on to the scene. Surely this is authorial intrusion, and of the worst sort.

Equally there is "authorial intrusion" when Huck decides to ignore the promptings of his consciousness and go to Jim's rescue. For the author is addressing the reader through Huck, and is saying something very different from what Huck is saying. Huck believes that in deciding to rescue Jim he is committing wrong, while Twain wishes to point out to us that Huck is not committing wrong, and that his so-called inner conscience is in reality only the arbitrary social values of his society. The fact that Twain does not break through Huck's point of view and tell us this himself does not in the slightest diminish the abundant fact of his presence during the scene, and our awareness of that presence.

To point up the difference between these two examples of authorial presence in *Huckleberry Finn,* we might say that in the episode describing Huck's decision to rescue Jim, the author intends that we know he is there; he wants us to see his point about the nature of conscience. At the outset of the episode at Phelps Farm, however, he has no such intention; surely he does not wish us to see him wrenching his plot and the laws of fictional probability in order to effect an ending for his novel. This distinction is quite proper in this instance, but talking in terms of what the author intends is dangerous business. Twain intended, for example, for *Joan of Arc* to be his best book, but this only tells us something about the author, not the book.

Let us go at it another way. Twain's presence in the conscience episode is an indispensable, integral part of the way it is told to us; the episode, in order to deliver its full meaning, requires our knowing what the author has to tell us about Huck's conscience. The authorial presence, then, is as much a part of the fiction as Huckleberry Finn himself is. Its function is formal, esthetic. The author's presence in the episode in which we learn that Tom Sawyer is momentarily expected at Phelps Farm, however, is surely not necessary and functional to the way the novel is being told. It is indeed an intrusion, distracting from the story and its meaning, impeding the flow of the narrative, severely trying our belief in the storyteller's artistic truthfulness. Tom doesn't *belong* at Phelps Farm; the coincidence is wildly improbable. The spectacle of Samuel L. Clemens figuring out a way to end his novel by reintroducing Tom Sawyer is very different from that of Mark Twain instructing us about Huck's conscience through and above Huck Finn a bit earlier; and different, too, from that of Cervantes poking fun at his imaginary Cide Hamete Benengeli and the supposed truth of fiction by having his characters talk about the book in which they appear. In the latter instance we have only a kind of humorous confirmation of what we have known all along, that the story is being told to us, and with the paradoxical result that the characters themselves are made to seem part of the telling, rather than the story.

The difference is formal, functional; it is the difference between fiction and biography. The authorial presence in the one instance is an artistic instrument, a formal device, while in the other it is biographical, unrelated to the fiction. In the conscience episode it is Mark Twain, teller of the tale, whose presence we sense; in the Tom Sawyer episode it is Samuel L. Clemens working his plot around so that he can resume his storytelling role as Mark Twain. One, in other words, is what Wayne Booth, in *The Rhetoric of Fiction*, calls the implied author, the same kind of voice as that which told us what Strether was later to decide about how he felt and acted when he came upon Chad Newsome and Mme. de Vionnet. The other is the biographical, real-life author, not part of the fiction at all, but having to do with the circumstances under which the book was written.

The implied author, the authorial personality who tells the story, can take many forms and can be present much more dramatically in some novels than others. In *Remembrance of Things Past*, for example, he is first-person narrator as well as author, while in *Ulysses* he is omniscient and never present in the action. But in both those novels he is there at all times. Is he Marcel Proust? Is he James Joyce? In *Remembrance of Things Past* he calls himself by the author's name—but we know that important differences exist between that narrator's life and personality and that of the Marcel Proust who wrote the novel.

In *Ulysses* the author's name is never mentioned—but if we know anything about James Joyce's life we can often spot some important resemblances.

What then is the identifying characteristic of the authorial personality, and which distinguishes him from the biographical, real-life author? Simply that the authorial personality is, whether dramatized as a first-person participant (and many first-person narrators are not authorial personalities at all, as for instance the Governess in James's *The Turn of the Screw*) or existing only in the way the story is developed and the language used to tell it, formally a part of the novel. The real-life author, on the other hand, is outside the novel, and can be reached only through biographical inquiry.

Sometimes, of course, the two may seem to come very close to being one and the same. Mark Twain talking about Huck Finn's conscience is also Samuel Clemens talking about himself as a child growing up in Hannibal, Missouri, and apologizing for once having accepted the divine right of slavery without question. But the one is part of the development and meaning of the novel; the other is biographical, nonfictional, unrelated structurally or esthetically to the artistic truth of the novel. A novelist may thoroughly dramatize himself, as a fictional character, without doing violence to the real-life image he has of himself, or even that his friends and acquaintances may have of him. Stendhal is an example of this; Henri Beyle made himself into a work of art, and the novels he wrote under the pseudonym of Stendhal are adjuncts of that artistic role. As Stendhal he is, in the role of authorial personality, an important formal ingredient of the structure of *The Red and the Black* and *The Charterhouse of Parma*.

Yet no matter how closely the two authors may coincide, they are not the same persons. The one is literary and formal, a characterization created by the author, while the other is biographical and historical. It is with the author who is part of the fiction, the implied author, that the chapters which follow will be concerned. I want in this book to explore some of the ways in which the authorial personality can function, and what they mean to the way in which we read works of fiction.

When at the close of *Don Quixote* Cide Hamete Benengeli prepares to hang his goose quill pen onto its rack, he pens a final apostrophe to Don Quixote and to his book. "For me alone Don Quixote was born and I for him," he declares. "His was the power of action, mine of writing." The Knight of the Woeful Countenance is dead now, and may no impostor seek to disturb his weary and mouldering bones. The purpose for which he was created has been accomplished. "For my sole object," the author concludes, "has been to arouse men's contempt for all fabulous and absurd stories of knight errantry, whose credit this tale of my genuine Don Quixote has already shaken, and which will, without a doubt, soon tumble to the ground. Farewell." [14]

Was that the object of *Don Quixote?* Cide Hamete Benengeli says it was, and perhaps that was Miguel de Cervantes' only object as well. Some Spanish literature scholars insist on it, while others disagree. But whatever the historical Cervantes intended, that is not what the man who so skillfully tells us the ingenious story of Don Quixote and Sancho Panza accomplished. That man tells us about brave men charging windmills, and changing barber's bowls into knightly helmets, and about reason in madness and beauty in folly.

When the Canon of Toledo questions the efficacy of knight errantry, Don Quixote replies with a lengthy defense of his pro-

14. *Don Quixote*, p. 940.

fession, in the course of which he delivers himself of these words:

> I can say of myself that since I became a knight errant I have been valiant, courteous, liberal, well-bred, generous, polite, bold, gentle and valiant, and an endurer of toils, imprisonments and enchantments. And although for the last little while I have been imprisoned in a cage like a madman, I expect by the valour of my arm, if Heaven favors me and fate is not against me, to find myself in a few days king of some kingdom, in which I can display the gratitude and liberality enclosed in this bosom of mine.[15]

The author who placed those words in Don Quixote's mouth is the personality whose presence pervades every page of his great tale.

---

15. *Ibid.*, p. 442.

TWO · The Novelist as Virtuoso: Stendhal

IGNORED by most French literary figures during his lifetime, Henri Beyle, who wrote under the pen name of Stendhal, died in 1842 in Paris. Only three men attended his funeral. Yet his novels, rediscovered shortly afterward, soon became classics, and nowadays so astute a critic as Martin Turnell, for one, believes him incomparably the greatest of all French novelists. "The originality of his vision and the discovery of a new psychological type have altered the whole perspective of European psychology and given him his immense stature," Turnell declares. "He is one of the most civilized of all French novelists and he seems to me to be the greatest." [1] Stendhal, says Allen Tate, was a novelist "whose typical heroes are persons of mere energy and whose books achieve whatever clarity and form that they do achieve as an accident of the moral ferocity of the author." [2] To achieve through accidental moral ferocity what critics such as Turnell say Stendhal achieved would seem to be quite a feat. How, precisely, one wonders, did he do it?

I want to begin my examination of certain authorial personalities with Stendhal, because in matter of strict fictional techniques—according to modern critical standards of what fictional technique should be—his way of writing a novel *is* fairly crude.

1. Martin Turnell, *The Novel in France* (New York, 1951), p. 208.
2. Allen Tate, "Techniques of Fiction," in *On the Limits of Poetry* (New York, 1948), p. 136.

He wrote with considerably less regard for the purities of narrative form than he might have done had he lived and written later in his century. As a principle of construction he thrust himself blatantly into his story, and he thus affords us the opportunity to observe how the authorial personality functions in the novel when it is set forth unashamedly and, as it were, naïvely (and narrative technique is perhaps the only way in which one might ever refer to anything about Stendhal as being naïve). What is it that Stendhal has to offer the modern reader, and how does he go about the practice of his craft?

In Stendhal's novel *The Red and the Black*, Julien Sorel, a young peasant who has been employed as tutor in the household of the Mayor of Verrières, dares to enter the chamber of his employer's wife and make love to her. Afterward, triumphant, he returns to his own room. "My lord, to be happy, to be loved, is that all it is?" he thinks at once.[3]

When the reader encounters those words, if he is familiar with Stendhal, he recognizes the sentiment at once. "N'est-ce que ça?" "Is that all it is?" "Is there no more to it than that?" At supposedly crucial moments in the lives of Stendhal's heroes and heroines—the first exposure to enemy fire, the loss of virginity, the arrival for the first time at a great city, one's first sight of corpses on a battlefield, one's feelings upon crossing the St. Bernard Pass, one's first entrance into a fashionable drawing room, this is the appropriate sentiment. "Is there no more to it than that?" Those human experiences which according to all that we read or are taught are supposed to mean the most to us, to be the most momentous, are upon us so quickly and so casually that they mean little or nothing. There is not so much

3. Stendhal, *The Red and the Black*, trans. Charles Tergie, Doubleday Dolphin ed. (New York, *n.d.*), p. 85.

disappointment as surprise, chagrin even; before one has time even to think about the importance of what is going on, one is accustomed to it. Only afterward, in retrospect, can the experience take on importance and meaning. Life is not so much to be lived as to be relived.

This is the way of Stendhal, and it is one of the charms of Stendhal. It is to be encountered not only in *The Red and the Black* and *The Charterhouse of Parma,* Stendhal's two most important books of fiction, but throughout his other work as well. The sentiment is drawn from his own life. As such, it is greeted by the connoisseur of Beyleism—Stendhal's own term—who encounters it here and there in Stendhal's work with the pleasure of recognition. For, as in the work of Proust, there runs through Stendhal's work a number of leitmotifs, which are at once recognized and enjoyed by the reader who is familiar with the Stendhal canon.

Much of the enjoyment of Stendhal lies in these moments. And since Stendhal is a highly enjoyable novelist, I want to try to show how his art functions, and what there is about Stendhal's way of telling a story that makes him so excellent, and so unusual, a writer. It has to do, I think, with the nature of his personality, and I believe that the way in which this personality operates has a great deal of bearing on the structural properties of Stendhal's work. There is a kind of novel, in short, in which the revealed personality of the author is vital to the way in which one reads the novel, and of which Stendhal's novels are representative.

The reader who begins a Stendhal novel for the first time, of course, will not recognize such moments as those described above, in which he encounters one of the Stendhalian leitmotifs. For this reader *The Red and the Black,* or for that matter *The Charterhouse of Parma* too, is likely to seem a curious book.

Julien Sorel is interesting, a most amusing young man, in fact; and many of his adventures are highly diverting, but compared to a novelist such as Flaubert, say, Stendhal seems almost an amateur. One has a constant awareness of the presence of the author composing his novel; Stendhal seems to be showing off, delivering himself of a virtuoso performance. What of that long conspiracy scene toward the end, in which the Marquis de la Mole brings Julien to a meeting of royalist conspirators, and after memorizing what has been decided, Julien goes off to deliver the message to a certain Duke? It contains some highly amusing political satire, it is an extremely funny scene, but what is its role in the novel as a whole or in Julien's development? Should the incident not have been either drastically cut, or else worked into the overall story much more effectively? It seems to stand there, alone, without being especially relevant to anything in the plot.

Yet the scene somehow works; and the novel as a whole is quite satisfying. The apparent formal deficiencies do not seem to matter very much. One way or another, Stendhal brings it off. What an altogether unorthodox novelist, this Henri Beyle, who calls himself Stendhal!

This then is how many a reader of *The Red and the Black* feels upon his first acquaintance with the novel (and it is this novel, rather than *The Charterhouse of Parma*, that the average reader is likely to encounter first). To the devotee of Stendhal, however, no such objection is likely to arise. Instead, in the conspiracy scene he is able to recognize, and to enjoy, many a witty thrust, many an allusion to men and events of whom he knows, and example after example of Stendhal being amusing, sardonic, indignant, appreciative, and so forth, in the kinds of situations and with the kinds of characters he is constantly thinking about and dealing with. The Marquis, for example, delivers himself, during the course of a long harangue, of these words: "Well, gentlemen, our heads are at stake. Between the liberty of the press and our existence as the nobility there is war to the death. You must either become manufacturers or peasants, or shoulder your muskets." [4] In the exaggeration of that bit of rhetoric—which is not really very realistic dialogue for such an occasion—there speaks, not so much an ultra-royalist nobleman who wishes to overthrow the precarious government of late Restoration France, as Stendhal himself, ironically putting forth the true issue as it might be phrased by his political opponents (for politically Stendhal was a liberal), in that daring, humorous way he has of stating these things. It is Stendhal at his best; the affairs of Julien Sorel are at that moment quite secondary.

It is for the devotees that the Stendhal novels seem designed. More so than most novels do the Stendhal books invite the attention of the reader who is willing not merely to read them once and be done, but who will return to the novels, and read them again in the light not only of having already once read them through, but preferably with the additional experience of having read Stendhal's other writings. Thoroughly to enjoy *The Red and the Black*, one ought to know the *Charterhouse*, and the *Life of Henri Brulard*, and preferably *Lamiel* and *Lucien Leuwen* as well. Nor need one stop there; there are also the *Private Diaries*, the *Memoirs of an Egotist*, the letters, the travel books and the biographies of musicians, the history of painting in Italy, *Racine and Shakespeare*, and so on, and so on.

Few readers will be able to bring all of that experience to bear on a Stendhal novel, of course, but I would wager that a surprisingly large number of people who have read one Stendhal novel have gone on to acquaint themselves with some of the

4. *Ibid.*, p. 363.

other material. This is not merely a tribute to the popularity of those novels; it is a descriptive statement about the kind of writer Stendhal is and the kind of novels he writes. His novels, in short, are *designed* to attract attention to their author, and it is not simply that they are interesting, but the particular way in which they are, that sends readers in search of biographical and nonfictional material about their creator. The central figure in the Stendhal novels is the author. It is the personality of the man who is moving Julien Sorel and Mathilde de la Mole and Fabrizio del Dongo and Conte Mosca and the Sanseverina and so on through the pages of the novels. The novels are written in a way that makes us highly conscious of and curious about the personality of the author. And to try to decide what manner of novels *The Red and the Black* and *The Charterhouse of Parma* are, without taking into account their relationship with the authorial personality, is to fail in fully understanding one's own experience in reading the Stendhal novels.

There is a point in *The Red and the Black* in which Julien Sorel, noticing that his employer's daughter is attired in mourning garb, and wishing to discover the reason for it, consults an Academician who he thinks will know the answer. "He approached the latter," Stendhal tells us, "as he was passing into the garden, and shared his anger at the success of 'Hernani.' " [5] The reference is to the Victor Hugo play which, when it was produced in 1830, was the occasion of rioting between supporters of the new Romanticism and those who favored the older neoclassicism. The furor contained distinct political overtones, for it was the young Liberals who came to cheer and the ultra-royalists who greeted each performance with howls and catcalls. Unless we know what was involved in the success of

5. *Ibid.*, p. 292.

"Hernani," we will miss the fact that Julien, whose private sympathies are all with its supporters, is, as throughout the novel, masking his real feelings in order to make his way in the ultra-royalist society upon which he is dependent for advancement. Again the reader is aware that Stendhal is doing this manipulating; the episode is a witty thrust at the status quo by the author, and intended to be recognized as this.

The important thing to remember is that we are not necessarily concerned with the real-life author of *The Red and the Black*, so much as with the implied author—the personality who is telling the story of Julien Sorel. The failure of most Stendhal scholars to recognize and appreciate that there is this difference between Stendhal, the authorial personality, and Beyle, the biographical author, is why Robert M. Adams can say with justice that "for all that has been written about him, it is curious how little has been done to estimate the literary stature of Henri Beyle, who liked to call himself the Baron Stendhal," and why Mr. Adams felt it incumbent upon himself to address his recent book to the question of whether Stendhal is "one of those writers who have slid into a major literary reputation through a series of fascinating but basically non-literary considerations." He asks this question: "Is he, in fact, a great novelist or a great . . . character?" [6] Stendhal has indeed been the object of intensive biographical inquiry; the "papers" of the famous Stendhal Club are commonly devoted to these matters. Yet this concentration upon author rather than novel is in itself a tribute to the success of the novels, and it may also point to the answer to Mr. Adam's question. For more than the novels of most writers, Stendhal novels draw attention to their author, and are great novels precisely *because* they display the personality of a

6. Robert M. Adams, *Stendhal: Notes on a Novelist* (New York, 1959), pp. xi–xii.

great character, constantly present and directing the course of events. Allen Tate furnishes us a clue when he speaks of the novels as achieving their form because of "the moral ferocity of the author." It is the "moral ferocity" of the author that gives form and clarity to *The Red and the Black* and *The Charterhouse of Parma*. But that author is not Henri Beyle, the biographical, real-life author, so much as the authorial personality to whom we respond as we read the novels.

To understand better the extent to which this authorial personality gives form to *The Red and the Black,* consider again the conspiratorial scene. Strictly from the point of view of the development of Julien Sorel, the conspiracy episode is largely irrelevant. It is not foreshadowed or anticipated by previous events. Julien has no hint that any such thing is going on; the conspiracy is simply brought onto the scene all at once, and Julien is placed in it. As already noted, the political and social satire involved has the effect of making us forget about Julien; he becomes important again only when the meeting is concluded and he is entrusted with the task of carrying the message to the Duke of X. But what happens then? Julien delivers the message, after encountering some difficulties en route, and thereupon the episode is ended. We hear nothing further about the conspiracy; it works no change whatever in the fortunes of Stendhal's characters.

By all rights, then, the reader of *The Red and the Black* might be expected to become annoyed by the scene, feel himself thrown off the track, and perhaps lose patience with the novel altogether. But does he? Not at all. Instead he will probably enjoy the episode thoroughly. This is because, while the conspiracy scene may mean relatively little to the fortunes of Julien Sorel, it means a great deal as far as the authorial personality who has been taking us through the novel is concerned; and if we have read that far along in *The Red and the Black,* we have fallen so much under the spell of the authorial personality that it is his commentary, and not Julien by himself, that provides much of the novel's unity and development.

Julien exists, in short, not only to have his adventures, to struggle for a place in the world and finally to fail, but also to permit Stendhal to comment on that world. These two developments—Julien's rise and fall, and Stendhal's interpretation of it —give *The Red and the Black* its shape and its form. The meaning of the novel resides in the manner in which those two developments work together. They cannot be considered separately; each depends upon the other.

The Red and the Black has with reason been called a splendid example of the political novel. Irving Howe, writing with this genre in mind, remarks that the book "constantly stresses the contrast between the loathesomeness of the society through which Julien Sorel must rise and the heroic spontaneity of the lost Napoleonic age," [7] a contrast that is even today fraught with meaning for French politics. In this respect, however, it is perhaps less satisfactory than *The Charterhouse of Parma,* which not only implies the same kind of contrast but also sets up as part of its plot the actual mechanics of government of a principality, and creates in the person of Conte Mosca a fascinating master of the uses of political power. *The Red and the Black* is less concerned with the workings of government than with the condition of a society. Since that society is the France of the Bourbon Restoration, part of the novel's attraction for us is historical. Indeed, Stendhal intended it that way; he wrote, as he frequently pointed out, not for his contemporaries but for

7. Irving Howe, "Stendhal: The Politics of Survival," in Victor Brombert ed., *Stendhal: A Collection of Critical Essays* (Englewood Cliffs, N.J., 1962), p. 79.

the more enlightened readers of a future time. Occasionally in his diaries and other jottings, he feels compelled to explain references to the contemporary scene in order that the reader of 1880 will be able to understand them. And in the *Life of Henri Brulard* he makes a statement echoed, with variations in the date, on various other occasions: "As for me, I am taking a ticket in a lottery in which the first prize amounts to this: to be read in 1935." [8]

But it is not simply that he expects his characters' exploits to indicate for future readers the state of society in his own time; he is also very concerned with pointing out the meanings himself. The presence of Stendhal is never missing from his novels. He is always there, setting up situations that will enable him to display his insights. When Stendhal assures us, as he often does, that he is primarily concerned with "the truths of the human heart," this is only part of the truth; to be more exact, as a novelist he is interested in performing his role in *pointing out* the truths of the human heart. He is, in other words, bent upon playing a part.

In one sense all of Stendhal's novels, and his other writings too, are tours de force, in which the author sets up a series of situations and creates certain kinds of characters in order to make his points. As has often been remarked, there is a peculiar kind of openness to experience about the Stendhal novels. Events do not occur, as they do in a Henry James novel, because they are the inevitable result of other events which have preceded them. Instead almost anything can happen, and often does. Why, for example, should Julien necessarily decide to enroll in the Jesuit seminary at Besançon when he leaves the De Rênal household? Why does he not instead go on to Paris? So far as the

8. Stendhal, *The Life of Henri Brulard*, trans. Catherine Alison Phillips, Vintage ed. (New York, 1965), p. 179.

actual plot of the novel is concerned there is no inevitability about this move, any more than there is an inevitability about Julien's leaving the seminary for the Hôtel de la Mole. Indeed, the denouement of the novel is not really inevitable, from the standpoint of the plot situation. When Julien's imminent rise to affluence and place as Mathilde de la Mole's lawful husband is suddenly and catastrophically blocked by the letter which Madame de Rênal sends to the Marquis, there is no sense of a remorselessly operating fate's having caught up with him at last. One feels as if it were almost a mere accident, which may or may not have occurred according to whether Julien's luck was running well or poorly. Almost *nothing* in the plot of a Stendhal novel is inevitable. The fight that Fabrizio del Dongo gets into with the actor Giletti in *The Charterhouse of Parma,* and that causes all the fond plans that the Sanseverina and Conte Mosca have for him to crumble abruptly, comes about as the result of an unimportant amorous diversion on Fabrizio's part, and the encounter in which he kills Giletti in self-defense occurs only because he chanced to be out in the countryside taking part in an archaeological project when Giletti and his entourage happened along. Even then, the event is allowed to ruin his career only because certain enemies of his aunt and the Conte desire to use it as an excuse for striking a blow at his benefactors.

What plot causality there is in both Julien's and Fabrizio's situations comes not from the inexorability of fate, but from Stendhal's view of the meaninglessness and viciousness of the milieu in which both exist. It is Stendhal's conviction that in post-Napoleonic Europe, a young man of talent and ambition must inevitably have a cruel time. As Julien tells the jurors at his trial for murder:

"I see men here who, without stopping to think of any allowance to be made for youth, would like to punish and discourage forever, through me, a class of young men who, born in a lowly station in life and borne down by poverty have the good fortune of becoming well educated, and have dared to mix up with what the pride of the rich calls 'society.' " [9]

This is Stendhal's theme in *The Red and the Black;* and in *The Charterhouse of Parma* the same is also true, for although Fabrizio is a young man born to a high station, his energy and his desire to Be Something and Do Something—he is not sure what —inevitably place him in conflict with the forces wishing to maintain the status quo, and in Stendhal's view something is then bound to bring him down. Julien loses his life; Fabrizio, who is essentially a less serious young man, loses his chance for true love. The price of his attaining the favors of Clelia Conti and the admiration of the public is the collapse of his integrity —which in Fabrizio's case is admittedly none too stalwart to begin with. In neither case, however, does anything which the protagonist does in order to gain his ends *cause* his downfall, in the way that what a Macbeth or an Oedipus the King does is bound to produce his downfall. Rather, Julien's and Fabrizio's actions are *used* to enable others to get at them.

The fictional development, then, comes not so much from the events of the plot as from the case which Stendhal is compiling against the purposelessness and vicious triviality of his times. This, even more than with Julien's or Fabrizio's careers, is where the buildup, the inevitability, occurs. The protagonists have their adventures in order that the author may in each novel exhibit a progressively more convincing indictment of a society without goals or ideals. Julien moves from the province to the seminary to the intrigues of the capital, and from the innocent love of Madame de Rênal to the complex histrionics of Mathilde de la

9. *The Red and the Black,* p. 457.

Mole, and finally to renunciation and death, so that Stendhal can at each step show what is wrong with the state of society. The same is true for Fabrizio.

This view of the meaninglessness of his times, of course, makes Stendhal give *The Red and the Black* and his other novels the curious openness of plot referred to before. So far as the careers of his heroes are concerned, nothing is inevitable, nothing inexorably causes anything else. Even the syntax of a Stendhal sentence, as Irving Howe points out, helps to reinforce this condition. In the Stendhal novels, Howe notes, "there frequently occurs a sentence structure that Stendhal had made his own: it begins with a limited statement and after an intervening colon or semi-colon proceeds to a second statement that is not so much a development from the first as an oblique or ironic comment on it. Ordinarily the colon is a bridge, here it is a chasm." [10]

The donnée in a Stendhal novel is usually the same: a young man (or, in *Lamiel*, a young woman) who possesses enough energy and ability to be dissatisfied with the status quo of post-Napoleonic Europe, is turned loose to undergo a series of adventures.

In *The Red and the Black* Julien Sorel, son of a provincial sawmill operator, is brought into the household of an upper bourgeoisie family as a tutor. He decides that his ambition requires that he seduce Madame de Rênal, the lady of the household. In the process he falls in love with her. When matters become too urgent, he departs for Besançon and study at the Jesuit seminary there. He wins the friendship of an ábbe, and this eventually secures him a position as private secretary to a wealthy and powerful Parisian ultra-royalist, M. de la Mole. So diligent and intelligent is he that he wins the confidence of his

10. Howe, p. 83.

employer, and also the favors of his employer's daughter, Mathilde, who finds his simplicity and purposiveness far more attractive than the charms of the wealthy young men of the Faubourg St. Germain. Julien is sent by the Marquis on a secret diplomatic mission, and when he returns he lays siege to the wayward affections of Mathilde. He is successful, and Mathilde becomes pregnant with his child; the Marquis, after blustering and threatening Julien, decides to endow him with fortune and station sufficient to justify Mathilde's marrying him. But just then the letter from Madame de Rénal arrives, whereupon the Marquis withdraws his consent, and the distraught Julien goes back to Verrières and shoots Madame de Rênal, wounding her in the shoulder. He is imprisoned and accused of attempted murder; both Mathilde and Madame de Rênal work to set him free, but Julien deliberately taunts the jury into finding him guilty, whereupon he is executed. Almost none of this action, to repeat, comes as the result of previous events. In fact, it is sometimes so little the result of probability as to seem almost unmotivated.

Why does Julien make so little effort to avoid his execution? Why does he in effect commit suicide? Because Julien realizes that only Madame de Rênal has loved him for what he was, and not for what he represented; Mathilde's love was occasioned by his symbolizing to her the strength and will power that she found otherwise lacking in Parisian society. All the way up the ladder he has been forced to dissimulate his true feelings. To gain favor in the de Rênal household he had pretended to a piety that he did not feel. In the seminary at Besançon he had won the admiration and affection of the ábbe Pirard when he was actually bitterly anticlerical and quite without any firm belief in God. At the Hôtel de la Mole he had pretended to be a young conservative, when actually he was anti-royalist. To

rise toward power and affluence, he has had to play the hypocrite. Why does he attempt to kill Madame de Rênal? Not because she has foiled his attempt to win wealth and the hand of
Mathilde de la Mole; rather, it is because her letter makes him
realize what he has almost succeeded in forgetting, that he has
betrayed his ideals. His immediate reaction—and this kind of
thing is why Stendhal has been called the first great psychological novelist—is *anger at her* for having made him see this
about himself. But as soon as he fires the shot, he is overcome
by remorse, and thereafter he makes no attempt to help himself. I am guilty, he says, and it is only right that I be punished.
Yet is he guilty as charged? He did not, after all, kill Madame
de Rênal. Nor was her letter to M. de la Mole really accurate;
Julien did not, as she had claimed, scheme to seduce either herself or Mathilde primarily in order "to be able to control in
some way the master of the house as well as his fortune." [11]
Julien knew this very well; his talent for hypocrisy did not
embrace his loves. Yet he let himself be killed when he could
easily have prevented it.

What really checks Julien, and makes him acquiesce in his
own execution, is the realization that in the society he lived in,
it was not possible for him to win fame and fortune, and at
the same time to retain his integrity and to love and be loved.
As Martin Turnell puts it, "his sensibility is exhausted. The extended personality has reached the point at which it can no
longer carry on, when there is nothing left for it in life." [12]
But why could not Julien have carried on, after being released
from prison and freed of the charges against him? Why is his
sensibility thus exhausted? Why, indeed, is Julien actually exe-

11. *The Red and the Black*, p. 427.
12. Turnell, p. 159.

cuted for his crime, when his intended victim was neither dead nor even seriously wounded?

The answer, it seems to me, comes down to the fact that the needs of Stendhal's commentary require that Julien die at that point. Stendhal wants to bring to a climax the truth of his contention, which is that in post-Napoleonic France there can be no place for someone such as Julien. To the young provincial, two careers were open. He could do what is friend Fouqué had wanted him to do, which was to renounce dreams of glory and come into the lumber business with him: in other words, become a solid middle-class citizen and devote his energies to the accumulation of money. Or he could seek power and fame through the church, which was the only avenue for pursuing these goals now that Napoleon was dead, the Empire gone, and a career in the military thus made meaningless. Either way meant, for Julien, the repudiation of his ideals, the suppression of his personality. In prison he finally realized this fully. And this was precisely the meaning of Julien's life as Stendhal developed it.

The episode of Julien in prison, his trial, his execution, was for Stendhal the last and most convincing illustration of his thesis about the absurdity of his times. The plot of the novel is constructed with that thesis in mind, and each event in its sequence was evolved in order to let him point this out. Look, he seems to be saying to the reader as the story unfolds, see the kind of thing that happens to a young man of talent nowadays?

It is, all in all, a highly self-conscious performance, in which the omnipresent author displays his wit, his wisdom, his irony. With that last dramatic footnote, in which Mathilde de la Mole histrionically proves herself worthy of her ancestor by carrying on her knees the severed head of her lover as the funeral procession journeys toward the mountain grotto which will serve as Julien's tomb, while the selfless, grief-stricken Madam de Rênal dies of a broken heart, the virtuoso undertaking of the Baron Stendhal is fittingly concluded.

This Baron Stendhal: never do we lose sight of him throughout whatever happens. He is, one might well say, Henri Beyle's greatest created character. Like Henry Adams, Beyle dramatized his circumstance, both to himself and to others. He too felt he had been born too late; when Napoleon fell, Beyle's career as man of action ended—not, as Robert M. Adams remarks, "gracefully or romantically, but with an awkward and satisfying thud." [13]

It was during the fifteen years from Waterloo until the July Revolution and the crowning of Louis Phillippe as King of the French, when Beyle was without influence or wealth, that his literary career began. After the Citizen King took the throne and the political primacy of bourgeois capitalism was formally recognized, Beyle received a modest diplomatic sinecure as consul at Civitavecchia, and depending upon his favor or lack of it with the Paris authorities, was able to secure leaves of absence so that he could live in Paris, where in 1842 he died. Not only the Bourbon Restoration, but, after the initial enthusiasm had gone, the bourgeois regime of the Citizen King was in his eyes a time when moneymaking and cant ruled, and men of ideals and integrity were automatically disqualified from successful careers. It is significant, I think, that all of Beyle's heroes are younger than he was at the time of writing; for them no Napoleonic period of glory and attainment had ever existed. They grow to manhood in a world devoid of excitement, glamour, and idealism. Again and again he returns to the same theme,

13. Adams, p. 8.

whether in his novels or his other writings: that in nineteenth-century France, passion, fervor, integrity have given way to moneymaking and the foolish social pretense of a society which is at bottom hollow and false. In the first chapter of *The Red and the Black* he tells us several times that the townsfolk of Verrières worship only money. Nor is Paris any better; "There is no more real passion in the nineteenth century," he has the Spanish Count Altamira say to Julien; "it is for that reason that people get so weary of life in France. The greatest cruelties are committed without cruelty." [14] "In Paris life is tired," he writes in *A Roman Journal,* "there is no longer any naturalness or free-and-easiness. At every moment one must look at the model to be imitated, who, like the Sword of Damocles, appears menacing above your head. At the end of the winter the lamp is short of oil." [15] Child of the Revolution though Beyle was, he looked back fondly and longingly on the Ancien Régime as the last period when genuine grace and passion were possible. As his friend Prosper Merimée wrote of him, "Beyle, original in all he did, which is a true merit in this age of faded manners, prided himself on his liberalism but was at heart a thorough aristocrat." [16]

Much of Beyle's fondness for Italy grew out of his conviction that post-Napoleonic France had become too calculating, too frigid for the man of fervor. Throughout *The Charterhouse of Parma* he conducts a running comparison of Italian attitudes with those of France, and customarily the Italian is superior. Yet though in his thirties he considered himself more Milanese

14. *The Red and the Black,* p. 285.
15. Stendhal, *A Roman Journal,* ed. and trans. Haakon Chevalier (New York, 1961), p. 330.
16. Quoted in Jean Dutourd, *The Man of Sensibility* (New York, 1961), p. 16.

than French, he kept returning to France, and especially during
the years as consul at Civitavecchia, he was miserable when kept
away from the Paris he affected to despise.

Beyle's response to his times was neither hypocritical acceptance, after the manner of his novelistic heroes, nor romantic
defiance; rather, as Irving Howe points out, it was ruse, "the
strategy of having one's cake and eating it, being both a rebel
and a *bon vivant*, deceiving society to undermine it and wooing
society to enjoy it." [17] He played a role; the man of wit, the
dandy of the salons, the passionate lover—"To me," wrote
Merimée, "Beyle always seemed convinced of the idea, widely
held under the Empire, that a woman can always be taken by
storm and that it is every man's duty to attempt this." [18] Yet
in the role of lothario, as he admitted freely in his journals and
diaries, he was far from enjoying a notable success. "The habitual state of my life," he wrote in *Henri Brulard*, "has been
that of an unsuccessful lover. . . . The fact is that I have possessed only six of the women whom I have loved." [19]

All this time, almost from the end of his Napoleonic days
until his death twenty-eight years later, he wrote furiously,
many hours a day—six novels, stories, biographies of musicians
and paintings, volumes of memoirs, guidebooks, journals, essays,
meditations, correspondence, reports. His complete writings, of
which only a small portion have been translated into English,
comprise seventy-nine volumes. What is most striking about
most of his work is not only its originality—and no matter how
much he borrowed from other men's books, he seldom failed to
make this material his own—but its wickedly ruthless honesty.
In an age of cant, it was his intention to write down the truth,

17. Howe, p. 82.
18. Quoted in Dutourd, p. 43.
19. *Henri Brulard*, pp. 15, 17.

come what may, which however much it may have caused him to be disliked or ignored by most of his contemporaries, would he felt, appeal to the readers of a future time.

Is there any other modern writer, save perhaps Emily Dickinson, who was so convinced that his audience was to be a future one, and that if it was slow in coming, it would also be sure? "I expect that in fifty years some literary botcher will publish fragments of my books which may possibly find favour as being free from *affectation*, and perhaps as being *true*," he wrote to Balzac when that novelist responded to *The Charterhouse of Parma* with the first real public encomium Beyle had ever received.[20] Throughout his work this theme runs. His books are dedicated "To The Happy Few," that select group of enlightened readers of the future who would understand the "truths of the human heart" and not be misled by pose and affectation. "I calculate," he declares in the *Memoirs of an Egotist*, "that my future readers are ten or twelve years old." [21] "So my confessions," he wrote in *Henri Brulard*,

will have ceased to exist thirty years after they are printed, if the *I*'s and *me*'s bore my readers too much; and yet I shall have had the pleasure of writing them, and of making a thorough examination of my conscience. . . . Morever, if they are a success, I stand the chance of being read in 1900 by such spirits as I love, the Mme Rolands, the Mélanie Guilberts, the. . . .[22]

His sense of himself as a creature engulfed in time, and of life as being not the changeless reality that the Christian of the

20. Stendhal, Letter, "To Honoré de Balzac," in *To the Happy Few: Selected Letters of Stendhal*, trans. Norman Cameron (New York, 1952), p. 366.
21. Stendhal, *Memoirs of an Egotist*, trans. T. W. Earp (New York, 1958), p. 1.
22. *Henri Brulard*, p. 8.

Middle Ages knew, but a process of constant flux, caused him to seize upon every opportunity to experience, understand, and record the present moment, and at the same time to watch with fascinated eyes the changes going on both within himself and in the society around him. This child of the Enlightenment— his beloved grandfather and namesake, Henri Gagnon, was a philosophe and friend of Voltaire—grew to manhood during the Revolution, saw and participated in the rise and fall of Napoleon, endured the confusion of the Bourbon Restoration, and spent his final twelve years of life as civil servant in the government of the July Monarchy and ironic chronicler of the triumph of the moneyed bourgeoisie. That one so much a part of change in his everyday life should find his consciousness dominated by the sense of the passing of time is scarcely surprising. His letters and diaries are filled with the rapt contemplation of time; he is constantly noting with fascination the changes in his own outlook. Indeed, the *Private Diaries* are heavily annotated by the author, who re-examined them on later occasions and pointed out to himself what had since transpired. Thus, for example, on July 27, 1810, he writes out several "thoughts to be read every morning upon awakening," consisting of advice about how to conduct himself. Then on March 13, 1813, he notes that this was wise advice because "I see more clearly into my character today," while on June 21, 1815, he again comments "precisely so. Instead of loving ambition, I've always been exasperated by what had to be done for it. Industrious solitude in a big city, GOOD FOR MY HAPPINESS." [23] And on certain momentous occasions, he feels compelled to note where he stands at the precise constant, as for example August

23. *The Private Diaries of Stendhal*, ed. and trans. Robert Sage (New York, 1954), p. 335 and *n.* 1.

3, 1810, when he learns that he had been appointed Auditor of the Council of State, and writes as follows:

> I opened this good letter at twenty-two minutes after eleven o'clock at night. I am aged twenty-seven years, six months and twenty days, having been born on January 23, 1783.[24]

His work is grounded in time, pervaded by the sense of its passage. There is no more moving and beautiful passage in all of Stendhal, I think, than the lines which open *The Life of Henri Brulard*. This novel, actually not make believe but a memoir of his youth, begins as Stendhal finds himself "this morning, the 16th of October 1832, at San Pietro in Montorio, on the Janiculum, in Rome,"[25] looking at the towers and ruins of the Eternal City, and thinking of time. "Ah! in three months' time I shall be fifty. Is it really possible? 1783, 1793, 1803, I count it all over on my fingers . . . and 1833, fifty. Is it really possible! Fifty! I am going to turn fifty. And I sang the air by Grétry: 'When a man is fifty years old.' "[26] He stops to take stock of what he has done and been, and he decides to write the story of his life: "then perhaps, at last, when it is finished, I should know what I have been, whether gay or sad, a clever man or a fool, brave or timid; and finally, whether the sum total be happy or unhappy."[27] There ensues a long, detailed account of his memories of childhood in Grenoble and his young manhood in Paris. At one point, discussing the years just before he left Grenoble for Paris, he writes this:

> My idea of beauty in literature is, in essentials, the same as in 1796, but every six months it becomes more perfect, or, if you like, it changes a little.

24. *Ibid.*, p. 337.
25. *Henri Brulard*, p. 3.
26. *Ibid.*, p. 4.
27. *Ibid.*, p. 6.

It is the *sole labor of my whole life.*
All the rest has been nothing but a *means of gaining a livelihood.*[28]

This perhaps is not quite accurate; Stendhal placed a great deal of weight upon love, and on *far' bella figura,* as his beloved Italians put it. Depending on his state of mind, he considered himself alternately a lover and dandy who also wrote, or a writer who diverted himself in society. *Visse, scrisse, amo,* runs the epitaph he wrote for himself at the age of thirty-eight.[29] "I have always written everything as Rossini writes music; I think about it, writing every morning what lies before me in the libretto," he declared in *Henri Brulard.*[30] His dedication to his muse was compulsive, continual, but it was not carried out at the expense of what the world commonly calls "a full and active life."

Stendhal's literary production, though voluminous, is fragmentary, incomplete; he finished only three real novels, and of them the first, *Armance,* is a decidedly lesser work. In addition to the superb *Life of Henri Brulard,* the wit and wisdom of the Baron Stendhal is distributed among a prolixity of unfinished novels, stories, memoirs, essays, biographies, diaries, manifestoes, letters, even diplomatic correspondence. The corklined room into which Marcel Proust retreated in order to master the meaning of his world has no counterpart for Stendhal. The unity which Stendhal was able to give to his writing was essentially the continuing unity of his personality.

All the same, we ought not to ignore the extent of that unity, or its formal, artistic importance. For in whatever he wrote, Stendhal's controlling presence is always felt. In the works of

28. *Ibid.,* p. 244.
29. *Memoirs of an Egotist,* p. 61.
30. *Henri Brulard,* p. 376.

nonfiction, there is never the mere documentation of the world; it is always Stendhal presenting and giving order to that documentation. Even so apparently factual a performance as the biography of Rossini is imbued from first to last with Stendhal's personality. It is not Rossini, so much as Stendhal on Rossini, that we read.

Similarly, *A Roman Journal's* fascination for us lies largely in the presence of the narrator and commentator—a performance, incidentally, which is apparently quite the product of his imagination, since he was not in Rome as he claims, but instead wrote it in Paris with material furnished by his friend Romain Colomb, and by using other guidebooks and histories.[31] Stendhal was an accomplished pilferer of material; but as he replied to charges that he had lifted whole sections from Carpani's book on Haydn for his own *Lives of Haydn, Mozart and Métastase,* "I would furthermore beg Signor Carpani to tell us whether he would make the delightful claim to have served as model *for the graceful style, full of sensibility without affectation, and not without pungency, which is perhaps the principal merit of M. Bombet's work.*"[32] The style makes the material Stendhal's own—forever transforms the material into art.

Those numerous pseudonyms—here he is writing as H. C. C. Bombet in defense of his brother Louis-Alexandre-César Bombet —are a clue, I think, to the unique quality of his work. They are devices for playing various roles, and he spent his life doing this. Everything he wrote, as well as everything he did, is part of the performance. Behind the performance there is the actor creating the roles, and it is he whom we watch as he does it. As

31. "Editor's Foreword," *A Roman Journal,* pp. 13–14.
32. Stendhal, Letter, "To the Editor-in-Chief of the *Constitutionnel,*" in *To The Happy Few,* p. 169.

Jean Starobinski writes, "Stendhal's good fortune as a writer lies in his incapability of leaving himself. In the reveries of metamorphosis in which he becomes Julien, Fabrice, Lucien, Lamiel, he changes face, body, social status, even sex, but it is always to tell his own life story while introducing greater fortune and greater misfortune." [33]

The unity, to repeat, is of the personality. But this is everything. For that personality, whether called Bombet, Beyle, Stendhal, Dominique, or any of the score upon score of names by which he went, is a created work of art. More so than with any other writer I know, the novels of Stendhal depend absolutely for their meaning on the successful projecting of the authorial personality relating them. Without the dynamic presence of that personality, the objective details of the plot of *The Red and the Black* and *The Charterhouse of Parma* would seem ill-formed, poorly motivated, arbitrary in development. But it is not only Julien Sorel's and Fabrizio del Dongo's adventures that we read; it is equally enjoyable to watch Stendhal as he makes them do what they do and say what they say. Critics who refer to these works as crude picaresque romances miss the point; they are no mere sequences of adventures, but unified works of art, with the unity residing in the authorial personality describing and commenting on the performance, at least as importantly as in the performers themselves.

This is why, to return to my first point, the true Stendhal devotee looks forward with pleasure to encountering, at key points in the Stendhal canon, those leitmotifs, those little phrases and comments, so uniquely and characteristically Stendhal's own, the essence of his personality and his art. "N'est-ce

33. Jean Starobinski, "Truth in Masquerade," in Brombert ed., *Stendhal*, p. 126.

qua ça?" "Is it no more than that?" Those who, out of a narrow conception of technique, refuse to grant the legitimacy of this authorial personality, who maintain that this personality has no role to play in really successful fiction, only deprive themselves of the rich satisfaction of Stendhal and of other novelists like him. This is not the biographical Henri Beyle who is making his presence felt, so far as the reader is concerned; it is the Baron Stendhal, a creation of that biographical Henri Beyle's imagination. This Stendhal so catches us up in the excitement and quality of his wit and insight that we straightway proceed to read his other and uncompleted memoirs, his diaries, his works of nonfiction, his correspondence, everything that he wrote or is reported to have said. In doing this we acquire a great deal of information about matters far removed from fiction—the consular service, Napoleon, the French stage during and after the Revolution, the politics of ulta-royalism and of Liberalism, the lives of painters and composers, the statuary of Rome, the way to take a respectable woman for the first time, the retreat from Moscow, the personality of Lord Byron, the superiority of Shakespearean drama over that of French neo-classicism, and so on. But it is never for these things in themselves that we read; what we want is to read Stendhal discoursing on these topics. For his genius is such that his personality pervades all he writes about; even a diplomatic report to his superiors in Paris reads like an episode in *The Charterhouse of Parma*.

If the Stendhalian personality is equally present in his non-fiction writings, one might wonder, why bother to read his novels rather than the nonfiction? And what makes the novels any more than his travel books and his memoirs, works of fiction? For the same reason, it seems to me, that the *Symphony*

No. 9 in D minor is more interesting, and so infinitely more creative a work of the musical imagination, than are Beethoven's *Seven Variations on "God Save The King."* Not only is there immensely more of Beethoven available in the Choral Symphony than in the piano variations, but however keen our pleasure in hearing Beethoven's musical commentary on a known and set theme, it is slight compared with a theme which is his from the start, and in which the development is not imposed from outside, but grows out of it and is so fused within the work that theme and development are as one. By analogy Stendhal on the subject of Rossini is delightful; but Stendhal on the subject of Julien Sorel is richer, more imaginative, more profound, because the character of Julien himself is the product of and an aspect of Stendhal.

Filled with insight and wit, steeped in the life of their times yet transcending their time to reveal the "truths of the human heart" that know no limitations of time and place, the Stendhal novels are memorable because they contain so much of the personality of the man who wrote them. So brilliantly is that personality created within them that those who read the novels are enticed to seek out his other writings in order to extend the privilege of knowing him. In so doing, they find that the other writings enhance the pleasure to be found in the novels, and they can return to *The Red and the Black* and *The Charterhouse of Parma* again and again, each time with renewed delight. It becomes a continuing process, from the novels to the other writings and then back to the novels; this is the genius of Stendhal.

Was the Stendhal who tells us these stories and who has written so many other interesting books a true likeness of the Henri Beyle who was born in Grenoble in 1783 and died in

Paris in 1842? And is the France of the Stendhal writings a true likeness of that country as it really was in the years after the fall of Napoleon? Or is the whole thing—fiction and non-fiction both—contrived to display the brilliance of Stendhal? How close, in other words, are Stendhal and Stendhal's times to Beyle and Beyle's times?

One could scarcely care less.

THREE · "Mark Twain Tonight"

B E T W E E N that urbane Frenchman known as Stendhal, and a former Mississippi River steamboat pilot who wrote under the copyrighted pen name of Mark Twain, there might at first glance appear to be much more difference than the breadth of an ocean and the passage of a half century of American and European history. One could not very well imagine Henri Beyle and Samuel Langhorne Clemens getting along very comfortably with each other, for all that they shared a taste for smutty stories; and even if time and geography had made this possible, it is doubtful that Livy Clemens would have encouraged her husband's intimacy with the gossiped-about French bachelor and bon vivant.

Whether Mark Twain ever read the novels of Stendhal has not thus far been recorded. Had he done so, however, he would probably have enjoyed them—though perhaps he might have disapproved of Stendhal's occasional excesses of frankness in print. The description of Fabrizio del Dongo wandering in-effectively about the fields of Flanders and later wondering whether or not he had actually been in the battle of Waterloo would have delighted the author of the *Private History of a Campaign that Failed*. As for Julien Sorel, one would hope that the creator of Tom Sawyer would have sympathized a little with the young provincial who mapped out his romantic campaigns with the help of books of Napoleonic strategy.

Both Henri Beyle and Samuel L. Clemens have in common a

trait which, for one who would study the role of the novelist in the novel, is quite interesting. Both men wrote under pseudonyms, and it is by those noms de plume that both are best known. This is not merely a biographical curiosity; it is indicative of the kind of writer each was, and the kind of novels each wrote. For the man who habitually uses a pen name must surely think of himself as playing a literary role; when he writes his book he is not Beyle, but Baron Stendhal, not Clemens, but Mark Twain. It is thus interesting that, however much their fiction differs, both men's novels are very much virtuoso performances. It is more than merely coincidental, I think, that both men tended to think of themselves as Characters, and that posterity has continued to regard them as such. Martin Turnell, for example, begins his excellent discussion of Stendhal in *The Novel in France* by imagining Henri Beyle holding a press conference. Mark Twain's enjoyment of the limelight is notorious. (How he would have delighted to know that a half century after his death the drinking glasses at the principal hotel of Hannibal, Missouri, would have imprinted upon them the legend "America's Stratford-on-Avon"!) Nor is it without importance that one greatly enjoys reading the minor, nonfictional jottings and writings of both men; the flavor of the personality who wrote the major works of fiction is also delightfully present in this material.

Stendhal and Mark Twain, in other words, were both great personalities, and much of the enjoyment to be found in their novels lies in the presence within books of the personality who wrote them. In the previous chapter I sought to show how the functioning of Stendhal as authorial personality is central to the way one reads his fiction. In Mark Twain's case I want to discuss how approximately the same kind of relationship works out in the achievement, and also the failures, of his best known book, the novel from which, according to Ernest Hemingway and others, all modern American literature derives.

Samuel Langhorne Clemens got into the fiction business gradually. He did not set out to become a novelist. He did not begin by writing short stories and gradually extending his range and his scope. Though the importance of his nonliterary, non-eastern Seaboard background can be overestimated, and often has been, his experience *was* greatly different from that of the other nineteenth century "classic" American novelists—Hawthorne, Melville, James, to name the only writers who can be considered as his peers—and his manner of writing novels was quite different because of this. He came East as a journalist and lecturer who wrote, and delivered in public, a popular art form known as Platform Humor. In certain respects he was not unlike a whole school of public Humorists who entertained the American citizenry with quaint, and sometimes instructive, anecdotes and tales about the Common Folk, and whose writings are today the tedious diet of American Literature professors and almost nobody else. Sam Clemens was better than the others—so much better that their importance today is mostly that of having contributed to the genre from which his talent evolved.

Growing up as he did not too far from the frontier, he did not have the disadvantage of having already read Jane Austen, George Eliot, and Anthony Trollope before beginning to write, nor did he have the advantage of having done so. The result was that he had to make his own mistakes, but also that he avoided some of theirs; and since he had a fine mind and heart, he discovered his own way to write literature. This resulted in books as wretched as *The American Claimant,* but it also produced *The Adventures of Huckleberry Finn* [*Tom Sawyer's Companion*].

In a brilliant book entitled *Mark Twain: The Development*

of a Writer, Henry Nash Smith, the foremost of Mark Twain scholars, has traced the way Clemens' literary art evolved from the western humorous sketches he wrote during the Civil War years to a point where he was capable of creating Huck Finn's epic battle with his "conscience," which as noted before is one of the great moments of art in America. Smith sees this development as a problem of technique, whereby Clemens progressively evolved the method that was to allow him to unite within a single coherent artistic image the vernacular culture of his origins and the "official" literary culture of his day.

What I shall have to say about *Huckleberry Finn* likewise has to do with technique, and draws heavily on Henry Nash Smith's insights. My concern, however, is not so much with how Clemens' art evolved to where he could write that book, or even with the achievement that *Huckleberry Finn* represents. Instead, I want to show something of how the novel depends for its accomplishment on the functioning of the authorial personality telling the story, and how both its success and its shortcomings are bound in with the way this authorial personality works.

For all that it is indubitably an American classic, *The Adventures of Huckleberry Finn* is today a very controversial book, and numerous and sometimes distinguished are the critics who have tilted lances over the novel—especially over the final section of the novel, having to do with the rescue of the Negro slave Jim from imprisonment on Phelps Farm. In that section, as noted in an earlier chapter, Tom Sawyer comes back into the story to join Huck Finn in the task of liberating Jim. Most critics agree that this produced a definite falling-off in intensity and achievement. Why it did, however, is another matter, and there is considerable disagreement about it. Henry Nash Smith analyzes the question very carefully, and concludes that Huck's surrender to Tom signifies Mark Twain's inability to discover any meaning to his protest against the genteel, traditional, Europe-oriented values of American High Culture. Huck's act represents, in other words, the virtual surrender of the Emersonian hope of a new nation peopled by human beings free of the errors of several thousand years of Western civilization. The glowing dream of Whitman, the craving of Thoreau for reality, the political vision of Jefferson and Lincoln, all are denied, or at any rate significantly modified, by what happens at Phelps Farm.

Poor Tom Sawyer is responsible. Or rather, the use that Mark Twain put him to is responsible, and his villainy comes because he represented what he did to his author. The author is very much present in *Huckleberry Finn*; even before the novel begins we get an explanatory note about the author's use of dialects, and a humorous admonition not to moralize about the novel. In the first paragraph we learn from Huck that he has previously appeared in *The Adventures of Tom Sawyer*, "written by Mr. Mark Twain," who "stretched things somewhat but mainly he told the truth." [1] Throughout the story Twain's presence is felt, and is important. Huck has at least three functions: he is a character, he is spokesman for the authorial personality, and he is the author's surrogate. But Tom Sawyer, as Smith points out, is in the Phelps Farm episode also the author's surrogate; Huck may be doing the commenting; but Tom is master of the revels, and very much to Mark Twain's delight. [2] Certainly the author himself never accepted the notion that Phelps Farm was what Bernard DeVoto has termed as "abrupt"

1. Mark Twain, *The Adventures of Huckleberry Finn*, intro. by Lionel Trilling, Rinehart ed. (New York, 1948). All quotations from the book are taken from this edition, and are given parenthetically.

2. Henry Nash Smith, *Mark Twain: The Development of a Writer* (Cambridge, Mass., 1962), p. 134.

and "chilling" a "descent" as ever happened "in the whole reach of the English novel." [3] Tom Sawyer's rescue of Jim was one of Twain's favorite passages in those public appearances he used to give; he delighted in reading it aloud.

We ought never to forget, when we are discussing Mark Twain's book, that he was by profession a public entertainer, and that long before he was a novelist he was a popular performer on the lyceum circuits. Very little of Twain's work is not meant to be read aloud, told to us, and this I think has some bearing on the way it is read today. We sense the authorial personality addressing us *through* as well as *in* what his characters do. Huck Finn is admirably adapted to the Mark Twain theory of telling a funny story, which involved the necessity of keeping a straight face at all times, no matter how humorous the passage being recounted. When Huck, for example, describes the circus at Bricksville, much of the success of the episode resides in the fact that he doesn't think the antics of the "drunken" bareback rider are funny at all; he is far too concerned for the man's safety. Part of the time Huck Finn is a "straight man" for Tom Sawyer, much of the time for the author. But he fulfills his various functions in various ways, and, so far as the reader is concerned, with very different kinds of results.

In his first spoken sentence, Huck says that only readers already acquainted with *Tom Sawyer* will know him, "but that ain't no matter." All the same, any inquiry into how *Huckleberry Finn* works ought, if only for reasons of contrast, to begin with a look at *The Adventures of Tom Sawyer*. We tend to write that novel off nowadays, and it is true, as Lionel Trilling says, that though *Tom Sawyer* has "the truth of honesty" and

3. Bernard DeVoto, *Mark Twain at Work* (Cambridge, Mass., 1942), p. 92.

that "what it says about things and feelings is never false and always both adequate and beautiful," *Huckleberry Finn* has both that kind of truth and "the truth of moral passion" as well; "it deals directly with the virtue and depravity of man's heart." [4] Still, *Tom Sawyer* was enough of a novel to make its author's reputation, and equally with *Huckleberry Finn* is likely to be read and enjoyed for many years to come. In T. S. Eliot's words, it is "a boy's book, and a very good one." [5] It is also more than that; it is also a book that adults can read and be reminded of themselves when boys.

Huckleberry Finn, on the other hand, is not a boy's book at all; a child is likely to miss most of the meaning of what goes on in it. I remember quite well that as a child the novel disturbed me, and Pap Finn's entry into the narrative at an early stage was quite enough to put me off: "There warn't no color in his face, where his face showed; it was white; not like another man's white, but a white to make a body sick, a white to make a body's flesh crawl—a tree-toad white, a fish-belly white." (p. 19) Though *Tom Sawyer* has gruesome moments as well, it does not seem to appal the youthful reader. In part this is attributable to the way it is told; it is told *by* Mark Twain, *as* Mark Twain, and not through either Tom's or Huck's consciousness. The presence of an adult authorial spokesman remembering and moralizing a little as he goes along sets up a temporal relationship that is never abandoned. The story is told to us as memory; we read it nostalgically. Furthermore, the authorial spokesman remains at all times outside of his material. He cracks jokes sometimes, and he tells us what to

4. "Introduction," *Huckleberry Finn*, p. vii.
5. T. S. Eliot. "Introduction to *The Adventures of Huckleberry Finn*," in Kenneth S. Lynn ed., *Huckleberry Finn: Text, Sources, and Criticism* (New York, 1961), p. 198.

think; he calls our attention to oddities and quaintnesses, makes sure we do not miss the humor of what Tom and his friends are doing, and generally performs much in the manner of a raconteur composing a story for an audience on the lyceum circuit.

But as Smith points out in his study of Twain's artistic development, late in the novel, when Tom and Becky are missing in the cave, Twain has to turn to Huck to keep his plot going, and in so doing, he discovers something:

. . . he had recognized the solution for several of his technical problems. It lay in using Huck as a narrative persona. The outcast Huck was far more alienated than Tom from conventional values. Telling a story in Huck's words would allow Mark Twain to exploit fully the color of vernacular speech. At the same time, the use of a narrator who was also a principal actor in the story would virtually compel the writer to maintain a consistent point of view.[6]

Indicative of this discovery, Smith notes, is the length at which Twain goes on with Huck's conversation when the necessities of the situation do not require it. Twain "has evidently become interested both in the workings of Huck's mind and in his speech; he exhibits him in the process of inventing a cover story—an activity that would become almost compulsory in *Huckleberry Finn*." [7]

The result is, among other things, that Twain's fiction is removed further from the ordinary conventions of the performing platform humorist, and closer toward the craft of the fully written novel. For he is able to show us not only what Huck is thinking, but also Huck as he thinks it, a distinct step forward in the creation of more complex characterization.

6. Smith, p. 90.
7. *Ibid.*, p. 91.

This is a very important development, but as Smith shows, the developing process did not stop there.[8] For in *Huckleberry Finn* there also ensues a striking example of the process which Mark Schorer has termed "technique as discovery." In early episodes of the book, when Huck hears what is going on, he reports the news to us directly. Even when his conscience begins lecturing him, the method of direct discourse is used. But later, and especially in the episode in which Huck decides to go to Phelps Farm and steal Jim from captivity, Huck reports such matters indirectly. The way he relates and interprets is thus made part of his characterization. Huck becomes less the mouthpiece for an authorial personality, and more of a character in his own right. His personality thus deepens as the novel progresses, and the result is a much more profound exploration of the meaning of the experience Mark Twain is describing.

What Twain does with Huck's deepened capacity for awareness provides both much of the moral force of the novel and, when it is abandoned, one reason why the Phelps Farm episode has been described generally as a falling-off in the book's power. Huck is able to triumph over his "conscience," that ingrained set of social standards masking as "morality" which tells him it is sinful to set a slave free, and to set his love of and loyalty to Jim over his civic responsibilities. "All right, then, I'll *go* to hell"—and he sets off to Phelps Farm. The shoddy values of the communities along the river bank—the divine right of human slavery, conformity, injustice masked as privilege—are thus transcended, and Huck Finn achieves moral insight such as none of the other townsfolk of St. Petersburg and the other river towns can know. So that, in Smith's words, "as Huck approaches the Phelps plantation the writer has on his hands a

8. *Ibid.*, pp. 120–22.

hybrid—a comic story in which the protagonists have acquired something like tragic depth." [9]

I want to discuss Phelps Farm at some length, because I think it important to the understanding of how the novel works, and the role of the authorial personality telling the tale. What is Huck Finn going to be able to do? More properly, how is the author going to be able to end Huck's story? He can have Huck set Jim free again, of course, but what then? They can take to the river again, and float on downstream, ever more deeply into slave territory, but that would eventually result in their drifting on out into the Gulf of Mexico, scarcely a feasible solution. Or they can try to make their way upstream once more, and by hook or crook connive to deposit Jim in free territory. This might be fine for Jim, but where would it leave Huck? Emancipated from the sordid compromises of society, he has no place to go. Tom's idea, stated at the end, that the three of them—Tom, Huck, and Jim—light out for the Indian country, would seem the only solution, but that frontier too, as Mark Twain himself well knew, would soon disappear. The only possibility would seem to be what in Huck's terms would be tragedy—acceptance of the necessity to conform to those very values and standards of nineteenth-century society he has so painfully succeeded in transcending. But this Mark Twain could not and would not accept; thus in the face of all fictional probability he introduces Tom Sawyer once again with "his intensely conventional set of values," and promptly converts the saga of Huck's and Jim's flight for freedom into a comic farce.[10] Thus the "chilling descent."

T. S. Eliot insists that Phelps Farm is the proper ending for

9. *Ibid.*, p. 133.
10. *Ibid.*, p. 133.

the novel, because "it is right that the mood at the end of the book should bring us back to that of the beginning." And, "what seems to be the rightness, of reverting at the end of the book to the mood of *Tom Sawyer*, was perhaps unconscious art." [11] It is this that so exercises Leo Marx, who declares that "such structural unity is *imposed* upon the novel, and is therefore meretricious," [12] and that "the return, in the end, to the mood of the beginning therefore means defeat—Huck's defeat; to return to that mood *joyously* is to portray defeat in the guise of victory." [13]

That is pretty strong language, but no stronger than others have used on the subject. Ernest Hemingway says the novel should have ended at the point where Jim is "stolen from the boys," by which I presume he means stolen from Huck by the Duke and the Dauphin, since Jim is never stolen from Tom. "The rest is just cheating," he says.[14] This is essentially the same verdict as Henry Nash Smith's, with the expatriate morality code added.

Meanwhile nobody has bothered to address himself to T. S. Eliot's question, which I think is a good one: "Or, if this was not the right ending of the book, what ending would have been right?" [15] Marx says only that between the author's Phelps Farm ending and one involving tragedy in its fullest sense, "there was vast room for invention. Clemens might have contrived an action which left Jim's fate as much in doubt as Huck's. Such an ending would have allowed us to assume that the principals were

11. Eliot, p. 201.

12. Leo Marx, "Mr. Eliot, Mr. Trilling, and *Huckleberry Finn*," in Lynn ed., *Huckleberry Finn: Text, Sources, and Criticism*, p. 208.

13. Marx, p. 207.

14. Ernest Hemingway, *Green Hills of Africa* (New York, 1933), p. 22.

15. Eliot, p. 201.

defeated but alive, and the quest unsuccessful but not abandoned." [16] He might have, but he didn't. And what is at stake isn't the business of rewriting a man's book; it is rather that if the ending of a novel is supposed to realize the final meaning of what comes before, then one way to find out what *Huck Finn* means is to decide what the ending means, and if it seems unsatisfactory, as it manifestly does, to decide what kind of ending would have been proper.

Let us agree first of all that the book shouldn't have ended tragically. Jim should not have been left in slavery, with Huck forced to give up his hopes of rescuing him. The whole, largely comic mood of the book is against that; even Leo Marx agrees that this is "probably" correct.[17] Neither Huck nor Jim, whatever their limitations, has a so-called tragic flaw; neither of them, that is, overreaches himself, neither deserves to fail, and neither brings on his own downfall through his attempts to avert it. Thus a strictly tragic conclusion, along Aristotelian lines, would be as unsatisfactory, because as arbitrary and illogical, as the Phelps Farm solution is generally considered to be. Aristotle's remark that the downfall of a virtuous man causes neither pity nor fear, but merely shock, is quite appropriate here.

As it is, the novel ends comically—but unfortunately the comedy is achieved at the expense of the deepening of Huck's characterization that has been going on up until then, and that has culminated in his remark that "very well, then, I'll *go* to hell." Instead, Huck stands by and helps Tom to treat Jim as a less than human creature, a stage darkie.

It should be remembered, however, that this is by no means

16. Marx, p. 210.
17. *Ibid.*

the first time in the novel that Jim is thus demeaned by his author. When the Duke and the Dauphin paint him blue and attach a sign to him saying that he is a "Sick Arab—but harmless when not out of his head," and instruct him to "hop out of the wigwam, and carry on a little, and fetch a howl or two like a wild beast" (p. 157), this may be a good way to keep Jim from being molested, but it is scarcely very dignified for Jim. The difference apparently is that at the time this scheme is necessary to safeguard Jim, whereas Huck knew perfectly well that the delay in setting Jim free and the indignities heaped on him by Tom while Jim is locked in the shed are not necessary. Still, there had been several opportunities, long before the episode with the Wilks family, for Twain to let Huck and Jim abandon the Duke and Dauphin and get on with their journey. Nothing prevented Huck from returning to the raft, or for that matter, from putting Jim and himself in the canoe and heading back upstream at night, leaving their newly acquired travel companions to their own devices.

Why did Twain not do this? Because Jim's quest for freedom had long since been subordinated to the pleasures of traveling downriver on a raft. In effect, Huck and Jim had chosen to seek the freedom of nature, of journeying along aboard a raft on the big river, and the plan to return Jim upstream as Huck's servant aboard a steamboat had been put aside, for the time at least. Only when Huck finds that the Duke and Dauphin have sold Jim into slavery again is Huck recalled to his original purpose so far as Jim's fate is concerned. Until then, in fact, Huck had never quite faced up to the situation; the downstream journey had been a way whereby he could put out of his mind the awful moral choice he must make—between his loyalty to his friend and his belief that aiding a slave to escape was sinful. Nor for that matter, if one looks at it this way, is Jim's position entirely without reproach. After all, Huck is not accompanying him in order to help him escape; he is fleeing from his father. Yet Jim knows, as we learn later, that Pap Finn is dead, and that the corpse he had told Huck not to look at aboard the wrecked steamboat *Walter Scott* was Huck's father. Should not Jim have told him that? Is not the fact that he did not tell him partly attributable to the fact that Jim knows that he will need Huck's help if he is ever to make his way to freedom?

Obviously the whole question of motives becomes ridiculous when viewed in this manner. *Huckleberry Finn* simply isn't that kind of a novel. The truth is that once Mark Twain lets Huck and Jim pass by Cairo in the fog and their raft moves downriver into slave state territory, they are embarked on a very different kind of voyage; Huck is no longer fleeing from Pap Finn, and Jim is not really fleeing from Miss Watson's captivity and the threat of being sold down the river to New Orleans. Only occasionally and briefly does either Huck or Jim remember the original objective. They are engaged in a voyage of discovery, and floating downstream becomes an end in itself. They are two rebels against society, and the various adventures they have along the shore are conducted much in the style of Don Quixote and Sancho Panza—though considerably more passively. The design of the novel during this phase is that of the picaresque romance; not for nothing does Twain tell us that Tom Sawyer much earlier sought to convince Huck that the Sunday school picnic was really Arabs and elephants in disguise, rendered that way by enchantment. At the time Huck had concluded that "that stuff was only just one of Tom Sawyer's lies, I reckoned he believed in the A–rabs and the elephants, but as for me I think different." (p. 14) Now for Huck the romance *is* real and believable. In true picaresque style, too, the forays he makes ashore point up the shortcomings and the fraudulence of the society of the river towns. Huck is "on the road," the road being the river, and the life he finds aboard the raft seems an enchantment come true: "It's lovely to live on a raft. We had the sky up there, all speckled with stars, and we used to lay on our backs and look up at them, and discuss whether they were made or only just happened." (p. 119)

The long idyll has to end, of course, and the question is how it is going to end. This much should be remembered, however: when Huck decides to steal Jim out of slavery, it is *not* with the intention of taking him back upriver and setting him ashore in free territory where he can send for his family. He doesn't even consider this. Instead, his object is simply to restore the conditions whereby the two of them can regain the river and resume their idyllic life aboard the raft. Huck's plan, as he tells Tom after that worthy has, in defiance of the logic of fictional probability, come upon the scene again, is to liberate Jim and "shove off down the river on the raft with Jim, hiding daytimes and running nights, the way me and Jim used to do before." (p. 233)

It is not Huck, then, who is in any dilemma at this point in the novel. He knows what he wants to do. Rather, the dilemma is that of the author, and it consists of finding a way to end the book. And before discussing the appropriateness of what goes on at Phelps Farm, we should first consider what things look like from the perspective of Mark Twain.

Scholars, notably Walter Blair, have demonstrated quite conclusively that *Huckleberry Finn* was written in three installments, over a period of eight years.[18] The first portion ends at

---

18. Walter Blair, "When Was *Huckleberry Finn* Written?," *American Literature*, XXX (March, 1958), 1–25. *See also* Blair's *Mark Twain and Huck Finn* (Berkeley, Calif., 1962), for a masterful study of the composition of Twain's novel, chapter by chapter.

the point when Huck and Jim, having missed Cairo in the fog, are drifting helplessly downstream, until the raft is run down by a steamboat. Until then, the emphasis has been on Jim's quest for freedom and his hope of making his way up the Ohio into free state territory. When the narrative resumes, that goal is forgotten. Instead Huck makes his way to the Grangerford plantation, to begin the series of adventures on shore and the interludes on the raft that culminate with the Wilks family episode and constitute Huck's and Jim's picaresque voyage downstream. When Jim is sold back into slavery, this portion of the novel is over, and we enter into the Phelps Farm episode.

During all this time, from Huck's earliest experiences with Jim, Tom, and then with Pap Finn at St. Petersburg and continuing on through his escape, his reunion with Jim, and the long trip downstream, Huck has been filling several roles. He has been a character, undergoing various adventures, and with a recurrently deepening insight and perspective. He has also, however, been serving as a vehicle through which Mark Twain can speak to the reader. He has been a narrative persona, and behind and through the persona stands the authorial personality of Mark Twain.

The extent to which Twain has been using Huck for this purpose should not go unnoticed. I have already pointed out how Twain uses Huck's naïveté and humorlessness for comic effect in describing the circus at Bricksville. This is but one, and among the less important, uses. Through Huck's eyes and with Huck's words Twain achieves numerous other purposes. He tells us about folk superstitions; he comments on the sickly sentimentality of the good folk of St. Petersburg; he criticizes sanctimonious cruelty and pious hypocrisy; he has Pap Finn deliver a fine tirade against the government and in the process show popular stupidity at work: he delivers some fine Negro comic performances; he satirizes popular tastes in home decoration; he pokes fun at sentimental poetry; he castigates the stupidity of feuding; he gets off some good satire on itinerant printers; he lambasts the credulity and sentimentality of evangelical religious attitudes; he pokes fun at Shakespearean diction; he shows the vicious sterility of emotion-starved communities along the river; he describes a wanton murder and then shows how craven and cowardly is a lynch mob; finally he satirizes maudlin sentimentality and gullibility in the Wilks family episode.

During all these episodes we remain quite aware of the personality of Twain as he manipulates Huck's consciousness to show us these things. To repeat, Huck often doesn't perceive anything humorous or vicious in what is going on, but this only adds to the comedy. Twain makes sure that *we* do. The authorial personality at these times is very much the platform performer, and in one episode, that of Colonel Sherburn's defiance of the lynch mob, Huck disappears almost entirely and Twain speaks for the moment through Sherburn himself, and very much to our awareness at that.

But Huck is more than persona sometimes, and more than character, too; he has a third function, one which we also grasp. He is the vehicle through which the author can take part in the story; he exists in a relationship of surrogate for the authorial personality. Twain places Huck in certain situations in which his reactions not only provide the opportunity for the unseen but felt authorial personality to make his points, but also enable him to identify his own feelings with Huck's. The reader senses a kind of imaginative kinship between Mark Twain and Huck Finn, a kinship very like that existing in so-called autobiographical fiction. I do not mean that Samuel L. Clemens necessarily underwent Huck's experiences when young; if he made any lengthy raft voyages, freed any slaves, and so forth, his memoirs and his biography do not record it. Rather, there are certain key incidents, recognizable to the reader, in which Mark Twain, the authorial personality, through what he has Huck do and think, places himself in Huck's position. Henry Nash Smith notes one such passage, just before Huck goes up to the farmhouse at Phelps Farm, in which Huck is overcome by melancholy. The associations that touch this off, Smith points out, are the "faint dronings of bugs and flies in the air that makes it seem so lonesome and like everybody's dead and gone; and if a breeze fans along and quivers the leaves it makes you feel mournful, because you feel it's like spirits whispering. . . . As a general thing it makes a body wish *he* was dead, too, and done with it all," (p. 219) and, a few lines later, the sound of a spinning wheel "wailing along up and sinking along down again. . . ." (p. 220)

Smith points to strikingly similar passages in the first chapter, in Twain's *Autobiography,* in *The Private History of a Campaign That Failed,* and in one of Twain's letters, and remarks that the association "strongly suggests that Huck's depression is caused by a sense of guilt whose sources were buried in the writer's childhood." [19] The depression appears at this point in *Huckleberry Finn,* he deduces, because it was here that Twain "was obliged to admit finally to himself that Huck's and Jim's journey down the river could not be imagined as leading to freedom for either of them," [20] and that therefore "he must withdraw from his imaginative participation in Huck's and Jim's quest for freedom." [21] Certainly, as Smith shows, Huck himself has no reason to despair, and anticipates no great diffi-

19. Smith, p. 132.
20. *Ibid.*
21. *Ibid.,* p. 133.

culty in liberating Jim from Phelps Farm. But in order to write the Phelps Farm chapters, Twain "had to abandon the compelling image of the happiness of Huck and Jim on the raft and thus to acknowledge that the vernacular values embodied in his story were mere figments of the imagination, not capable of being reconciled with social reality."[22]

This seems to me a highly sensible observation on Smith's part. How, though, can the reader of the novel who is unfamiliar with kindred passages in other writings by Twain which make Smith's case convincing, recognize the emotion being described as Twain's rather than, or equally with, Huck's? Because, I think, the intensity of the passage, the impact the experience has on Huck, is all out of proportion to the general level of his characterization. The kind of introspection described is extremely subtle, having to do with Huck's feelings, and most of the time Huck does not display that kind of subtlety or insight. When encountering such a passage the reader senses, therefore, that Huck is expressing his author's attitudes, and that these attitudes, however much the situation itself may be contained in the plot structure, come from Mark Twain's life and memories. The reader, I would emphasize, may not dwell on these matters, may pass them by swiftly, but the idea does cross his mind for the moment.

Are there other moments like these? I suggest that there are several at least. One is the highly lyrical, beautifully rendered description, after Huck and Jim leave the Grangerford plantation and just before they encounter the Duke and Dauphin, of the sights, sounds, smells, and the feeling of being adrift down the river on a raft. (pp. 117–19) Though Twain intersperses some humor about Huck's and Jim's naïveté and Huck's sense in

22. *Ibid.,* p. 132.

realizing that no spirit adrift in the fog would say, "Dern the dern fog," the general sense of the passage, the subtlety of observation, the complexity of the description, are not typical of Huck's normal level of discourse, however expressed in his language (though obviously Olivia Langdon Clemens' husband, not Huck, has substituted "dern" for "damn"). These passages stand out, in their lyricism and their insight, from Huck's customary ways of thinking and discourse, and especially in the passage just mentioned one marvels not only at the beauty, but also at the skill with which the author has managed to express what he does while limiting himself to Huck's vocabulary. In *Tom Sawyer* there are similar passages, but the omniscient narrator delivers them; in *Huck Finn* Mark Twain speaks through Huck, but he delivers them all the same, and the more successfully for the simplicity of the vocabulary he uses.

But there is another kind of passage in which Huck Finn becomes Mark Twain's surrogate, and which involves not Huck's occasional descriptive powers or subtlety at divining his own feelings, but Huck's moral consciousness. One of these I have already mentioned. When Huck engages in his famous debate with his conscience, writes a letter advising Miss Watson of Jim's whereabouts, then decides "all right, then, I'll *go* to hell," and tears up the letter, he is clearly serving as his author's surrogate.

The episode, which is so well known that I shall not quote from it, is dramatically very effective. It is also, however, and in another sense, quite programmatic. Mark Twain is not simply showing us Huck's decision to steal Jim out of slavery; he is also, and in considerable detail, making a point about society. He is demonstrating that a society's morality is social, not innate, and that, in Smith's words, "Huck's conscience is simply the attitudes he has taken over from his environment." Smith continues: "What is still sound in [Huck] is an impulse from the deepest level of his personality that struggles against the overlay of prejudice and false valuation imposed on all members of the society in the name of religion, morality, law, and refinement." [23]

That this demonstration is going on is quite obvious to the reader; and also, that not Huck Finn but Mark Twain is showing it to him. The authorial personality is at this moment very much addressing the reader through Huck, and the reader expects it and appreciates it. The telling contrast between Huck's deepest impulses of loyalty to his friend Jim and his commitment to the artificial moral convictions of his society is a dramatized social observation, imposed by Twain on his story.

Similarly, when Huck, concocting a tale about a steamboat explosion for the benefit of explaining to Aunt Sally his supposed delay in arriving at Phelps Farm, is asked, "Good gracious! anybody hurt?" he replies, "No'm. Killed a nigger," whereupon Aunt Sally remarks that "Well, it's lucky; because sometimes people do get hurt." (p. 222) We are likewise quite aware of the author's giving us a similar, if less sustained demonstration. This time Huck is apparently not emancipated from his society's value structure. But the author is clearly telling us that his characters were in their time and place oblivious of the Negro's humanity.

The use of Huck Finn by Mark Twain as spokesman and surrogate, then, is frequent in the novel, and the relationship thus involved is very much a part of the way the novel is told. I want now to examine what happens at Phelps Farm, with this authorial relationship in mind. I think that it can help us to understand what is wrong, and what is right, about the often disputed incident in which Huck, pretending to be Tom, and Tom,

23. Smith, p. 122.

pretending to be his half-brother Sid, stage their celebrated rescue of Jim from his captivity in the farm outhouse.

It will be remembered that by an almost unbelievable coincidence, the Arkansas farm on which Jim is imprisoned, and to which Huck comes to rescue him, trusting to providence to provide the way, turns out to be that of Tom Sawyer's uncle and aunt, and the aunt promptly assumes that Huck is Tom, who also by extraordinary coincidence is due momentarily on a visit. The reader's sense of fictional probability, as previously noted, is jarred at that moment. A more motivationally conscious craftsman than Mark Twain would have set up the matter more plausibly; this would have been fairly easy to do, perhaps by having Tom in the early pages of the story talk about having to visit his aunt and uncle in Arkansas, and then by having Huck think about this occasionally as he and Jim drift southward down the river, so that when Huck moves toward Phelps Farm it would have been with the knowledge that he would find Tom there. That, or something like it, would have diminished the reader's sense of the story being wrenched into shape to fit the author's needs. Still, one's sense of implausibility is soon dismissed, or at any rate discounted, for so strong is the spell of Mark Twain as storyteller that we do not object too strenuously or too long to such things. (Can, though, one imagine such a thing taking place in, say, Henry James's *The Turn of the Screw?* There too a storyteller is involved, but a different kind, and existing in a very different relationship to his story and to the reader.)

What happens structurally in the Phelps Farm incident is quite important, however. As Henry Nash Smith remarks, not only does Huck have to assume Tom's name, but more importantly, a decisive shift in authorial identification takes place, from Huck to Tom. "Mark Twain has found out who he must be in order to end his book: he must be Tom." [24] The quest for natural freedom on the river is over. To end his novel, Mark Twain must leave the downstream journey and invent a comic plot. And for that purpose, Huck will not do; his mind does not operate in the necessary fashion. The kind of imagination that Tom Sawyer possesses is more appropriate now.

Once Huck and Tom have gone off into the woods and have seen the Duke and Dauphin being ridden out of town on a rail, tarred and feathered, and Huck, with his great power of sympathy, feels somehow responsible, Huck ceases to be the central character, and exists chiefly to describe and to set off Tom Sawyer in action. Tom's thought, Tom's behavior, Tom's imagination become the focus of the story, and remain so until almost the end.

Because of the dropoff in moral intensity—the comedy at Phelps Farm is of a different and perhaps less attractive order than the theme of the downstream journey on the raft and the flight for Jim's freedom—most critics have tended to blame the presence of Tom Sawyer, or at any rate to see him as a distinctly inferior person. Not everyone would go to the extent of one recent commentator, Ray B. Browne, for whom Tom is no less than Huck's "evil genius," [25] but most readers would probably agree with Lionel Trilling's characterization of "the mind of Tom Sawyer with its literary furnishings, its conscious romantic desire for experience and the hero's part, and its ingenious schematization of life to achieve that aim." [26] Yet if Tom at Phelps Farm becomes what Huck has been up until that point, the authorial personality's surrogate self, how do we ac-

24. Smith, p. 133.

25. Ray B. Browne, "Huck's Final Triumph," *Ball State Teachers College Forum*, VI, 1 [winter, 1965], 11.

26. Trilling, p. xvi.

count for the sudden moral decline on the author's part, and
what does that make of Mark Twain?

The chief reason why Tom Sawyer has incurred the wrath
of some critics and the pity of other's is probably that he is
quite willing and able to subject Jim to considerable discomfort
and indignity even though he knows all the while that Jim
is really a free man, having been given his freedom by his
owner, Miss Watson, on her deathbed. Huck no doubt con-
tributes greatly to this judgment because of his amazement that
a respectable boy such as Tom would be so wanting in moral
responsibility and ethical uprightness as to be willing to help
him steal Jim out of captivity. When later we find out that Tom
has been willing to do this because he knows Jim is free anyway,
the apparent mystery is solved—at the expense of Tom's integrity, so far as his readers are concerned. "Tom," says Henry
Nash Smith, "is a comic figure in the classical sense of being a
victim of delusion. He is not aware of being cruel to Jim because he does not perceive him as a human being. For Tom, Jim
is the hero of a historical romance, a peer of the Man in the
Iron Mask or the Count of Monte Cristo." [27]

Precisely. But one must not stop there. Not only is Jim "the
hero of a historical romance" for Tom, but *so are Tom and
Huck.* They are all three storybook characters—in Tom's version of reality. Tom is quite as demanding of himself and Huck
as of Jim; we recall his lengthy attempts to climb back into
his room at night by the lightning-rod, because no storybook
hero would think of using the staircase: "after he got up half-
way about three times, and missed fire and fell every time, and
the last time most busted his brains out, he thought he'd got
to give it up; but after he was rested he allowed he would give

27. Smith, p. 134.

her one more turn for luck, and this time he made the trip."
(p. 236) No ordeal is too arduous for Tom, no labor is too demanding, provided that it is called for by the canons of romance.
And he is most pleased of all when in the confusion of Jim's
escape he is shot in the leg; proudly he tells Huck and Jim to
leave him and conclude the escape. A bullet in the calf of his leg;
what could be more perfect?

Tom is doing here exactly what he did throughout *The Adventures of Tom Sawyer,* and what he had attempted to do in
the early chapters of *Huckleberry Finn.* He is attempting,
through the use of his imagination, to convert the mundane,
limited everyday world of daily life along the Mississippi into
something involving glamour, excitement, and romance, with
the potentialities for heroism that apparently are not present in
everyday reality. In *Tom Sawyer* he succeeded in that; did he not
convert everyday life in St. Petersburg into a reality involving
buried treasure, pirates, thrilling rescues from underground
caverns, in which success, which involved fame and wealth, was
possible for him and Huck? Was not the aftermath that of caus-
ing "every 'haunted' house in St. Petersburg and the neighbor-
ing villages" to be "dissected, plank by plank, and its founda-
tions dug up and ransacked for hidden treasure—and not by
boys, but men—pretty grave, unromantic men, too, some of
them?" [28]

Tom is no ordinary citizen of St. Petersburg, any more than is
Huck; but while Huck's way of rebellion is through flight, and
the moral realization of Jim's humanity, Tom's is through imagination. For once I disagree with Henry Nash Smith when he
remarks that Tom has an "intensely conventional sense of

28. Mark Twain, *The Adventures of Tom Sawyer: The Complete Works of
Mark Twain,* I (New York, 1922), p. 285.

values." It is true, as Smith goes on to say, that Tom was "impervious to the moral significance of the journey on the raft,"[29] but Tom is nobody's conformist, and it is a mistake to portray him in that light. Romantic, melodramatic he perhaps is, but no more than Huck Finn is he satisfied with the way things are done in St. Petersburg and elsewhere along the big river. And be it noted that Tom once again succeeds in his imaginative transformation. Earlier Huck had found himself unable to believe that the Sunday school picnickers were really Arabs in caravanserai. Now Tom has won his friend's assent again, and Jim's as well. Skeptical though Huck was during the feat, he had gone along with it, and all had worked out well. Now to head for the Indian country and more adventures.

But Tom *knew that Jim was free* all the while. There is the rub. This is what spoils the sheer comedy of the great "evasion." And that, I suggest, and not the episode itself, is what is wrong with the Phelps Farm sequence as the way to end the novel. It was not Tom's romanticism, and not even Jim's discomforts— Jim didn't especially mind, any more than he minded being the Sick Arab during the Wilks family episode. Is Jim's character thereby debased, as Leo Marx says, in that the antics "divest Jim, as well as Huck, of much of his dignity and individuality?"[30] I don't think so, for the simple reason that throughout the course of the novel Jim has filled much the same role. The hair-ball incident, the superstitions, the debate about Solomon's wisdom, the discussion about the ways of kings and dukes and Jim's gullibility during the same—Jim has been used throughout for low comedy. His individuality has always resided in the way that from time to time he emerges through the stereotype to

29. Smith, p. 133.
30. Marx, p. 206.

show himself a genuine human being capable of loyalty and nobility. Phelps Farm is one more instance of that emergence: when Jim sticks with the wounded Tom instead of fleeing, and submits to rough treatment in order not to betray Huck, he asserts his moral identity once again. The point about Jim has always been that a Negro slave, uneducated, superstitious, naïve, childlike, can triumph over these environmental limitations and be a man. Phelps Farm confirms the transaction.

The difficulty, to repeat, is not so much that Jim is imposed on, but that Tom goes through with his romantic adventure when he knows all the time that Jim is free. To return to T. S. Eliot's question about how the novel should have been concluded if not in the way that Mark Twain chose, the answer may well be that Twain's mistake was in having Tom Sawyer know that Jim was already free. Had Tom not known, so that his conduct toward Jim would not have been sullied by his apparent willingness to use the helpless Jim as an instrument in his romantic comedy, the relationship of the Phelps Farm episode to the rest of the novel would be seen in much clearer terms. For it *is* a humorous episode, and Twain certainly did not intend through it to humiliate Jim. And if the great theme of *Huckleberry Finn* is escape—escape from the falseness, the hypocrisy, the sentimentality, the selfishness, the materialism of society, then the true meaning of Phelps Farm is that if any escape is possible it is possible only through the imagination, with all the attendant perils of isolation and alienation that such an escape involves. For Tom's great rescue, however much it pleased him, Huck, and Jim, was finally only a game, as fanciful as Alice's adventures beyond the looking glass, and as silly. *Huck Finn* is the same kind of novel as its model, *Don Quixote;* the Knight of the Woeful Countenance is like Huck in his sincerity and loftiness of spirit, like Tom in his ingenuity and imagination. No less than Quixote do Huck and Tom tilt with windmills. And no less than Quixote are both knocked sprawling for their pains.

The proper ending for *Huckleberry Finn*—proper because it would have embodied that final meaning—was for Aunt Polly, not Tom, to have known and at the end revealed that Jim had been free all the time. This would have provided the profound undercutting of the whole episode that would place Tom's efforts, as well as Huck's, in proper perspective. For the meaning of the book is the impossibility of escape from society and also the brave but futile heroism of those who attempt it.

Surely that is what the book and also its companion work, *The Adventures of Tom Sawyer,* meant for Mark Twain. The helpless rage of *A Connecticut Yankee in King Arthur's Court,* the despair of *The Mysterious Stranger,* are both foreshadowed by Huck's failure to find freedom for himself and Jim on the raft, and Tom's inability to make his great rescue possess any real meaning. "You perceive, *now* that these things are all impossible except in a dream," Satan declares before he vanishes in *The Mysterious Stranger.* "You perceive that they are pure and puerile insanities, the silly creations of an imagination that is not conscious of its freaks—in a word, that they are a dream, and you the maker of it. . . ." [31]

Why *did* Mark Twain undercut Tom's conduct by having him know that Jim was already free? Not because he wanted to portray Tom unsympathetically; Tom is otherwise treated with much affection (sometimes wryly to be sure) by the creator, which is not surprising, because Tom was a part of Mark. Twain found Tom amusing, greatly so; and he also found him impractical. Rather, it is because at that point in the novel Tom *was*

31. Mark Twain, "The Mysterious Stranger," in *The Mysterious Stranger: The Complete Works of Mark Twain,* VIII (New York, 1922), p. 140.

Mark when young, and Mark *knew* that Sam Clemens when young and a Missourian would never have stolen a slave from his owner. Sam Clemens was a product of his time and place, and he transcended them only when he had grown older, and through the medium of the imagination that Tom possessed. Tom, and Huck—for Huck is the young Mark Twain too, but as he might have been had he *not* been so bound to his society, so thoroughly schooled in its values. Huck, orphaned as Tom and Mark were not, unschooled and untaught as Mark and Tom were not, and therefore close enough to Jim to see him as a human being, was able to break through the moral limitations of St. Petersburg. T. S. Eliot is right when he says that Tom "might become Mark Twain. Or rather, he might become the more commonplace aspect of Mark Twain. Huck has not imagination, in the sense in which Tom has it; he has, instead, vision." [32]

But Mark Twain was both Tom and Huck, and that is why *The Adventures of Huckleberry Finn* is what it is: a classic of vision and imagination, but a classic that is flawed by its errors, which are those of the author. When Eliot says that "it is right that the mood of the end of the book should bring us back to that of the beginning," [33] he is wrong—and he is right. He is wrong, because the merely comic imagination of Tom Sawyer at Phelps Farm is limited by its moral insensitivity; and the hard-won moral vision of Huck Finn is thus mocked. He is right, because the contradiction was there, in the mind of the man telling us the story, and the book is the image of Mark Twain.

How can a novel be as good a novel as *The Adventures of*

32. Eliot, p. 198.
33. *Ibid.*, p. 201.

Huckleberry Finn is generally thought to be, and yet have so grievous, or in any event so incongruous, a conclusion as the Phelps Farm episode? The answer, I think, has something to do with the same reason that, in Stendhal's *The Red and the Black,* the apparent irrelevance of the ultra-Royalist conspiracy scene seems actually not to be irrelevant. In Twain, as in Stendhal, the presence of the authorial personality telling the story is structurally so important that the strict logic of plot development and character motivation cannot be narrowly applied. In the instance of *Huckleberry Finn,* however, this is complicated by something that is not a factor in *The Red and the Black:* an obvious wrenching of the plot to give the book an ending, and thus an obvious division in the personality of the author telling the story. Yet the principle is the same. The Phelps Farm sequence may represent an important change in the personality of Huck Finn, an important shift in the mood of the book. But what happens at Phelps Farm is not inconsistent with, though perhaps it is a less attractive part of, the personality of the author; by no means is it the first time in the novel that this side of Mark Twain has been evident. That he reverts back to the kind of humor that is featured in the early episodes of the book, and intermittently thereafter, is therefore not a complete break in the flow of the story. In another novel the reversion might have been disastrous; but in *Huckleberry Finn* we have come to depend so strongly on the author's performance that he is able, however less admirably it does not matter, to carry us through to the end. And when Twain returns, at the last, to being Huck again, and prepares to light out for the territories ahead of the rest because he is about to be civilized by Aunt Sally, not only he, but we as well, have been there before. Narrative consistency and the unity of plot notwithstanding, we will go along with Mark Twain wherever he chooses to take us, sentimentalities, inconsistencies, lapses of taste, and all. This is all a part of the novel, which in turn is the embodiment of the man.

From all the books, finished and unfinished, from all the sketches, narratives, and so forth that constitute his collected works, there emerges one great figure, no less interesting to us now as to his contemporaries during his lifetime: Mark Twain. No wonder Samuel L. Clemens copyrighted the trademark: that name was his most valuable literary possession. "Mark Twain Tonight," one recent platform artist called his show of readings of Twain's works. So it is each time we read *Huckleberry Finn*. We take delight in Huck, Tom, Jim, and in the personality of the great artist who tells their story. He is in his characters, and he is above and beyond and before them, always on stage. Attempting to sum up the reasons for the worldwide success of *The Adventures of Huckleberry Finn*, Walter Blair remarks that "the life, the thought, the complex personality of Mark Twain, given immortality here as nowhere else, also have tremendous fascination." [34] Also? Most of all is that Mark Twain whose name appears on the title page his author's foremost invention. Whenever we pick up a copy of his novel and begin to read, it is "Mark Twain Tonight."

34. Walter Blair, *Mark Twain and Huck Finn* (Berkeley, Calif., 1962), p. 384.

FOUR · The Presence of the Master

IT is one thing, perhaps, to demonstrate the existence and the importance of an authorial personality in the novels of Stendhal and Mark Twain. Stendhal wrote before Flaubert had begun perfecting the formal structure of the French novel, while Mark Twain came to the writing of fiction straight off the lecture platform and was never greatly concerned with the more subtle problems of fictional representation. But what of the novels of a different kind of writer than either, a writer whose greatest concern was with technique, and for whom the fine points of the art of fiction were always a deadly serious and constantly meditated business? What, in short, of Henry James?

It is safe to say, I think, that there are readers who might accept the idea that an authorial personality is part of the formal structure of many good novels, and yet who would insist that in James no such presence was at work. Henry James "dramatized" his fiction; he all but invented the notion of the so-called "effaced author." How then could his authorial personality intrude?

I want now to try to answer that question, through a consideration of the James novel that most readers know best, and that James himself thought his best and most perfectly formed work: *The Ambassadors*.

At least since Percy Lubbock and Joseph Warren Beach published their seminal studies during the 1920's, Henry James has been among the most thought-about and written-about practitioners of the novel in all twentieth-century fiction. The adjective "Jamesian" has become a byword for craft, applied to the novelist who is especially interested in the technique of his art. One could scarcely quarrel with T. S. Eliot when he says that "compared with James's, other novelists' characters seem to be only accidentally in the same book."[1] What most novelists glimpsed, or managed without being conscious of doing so, James recognized, articulated, and examined from all possible angles.

He was pre-eminently the novelist of dramatization, of scene-building. In essay after essay and book review after review, written over the course of a lifetime devoted to the art of fiction, and most notably in those enthralling, if somewhat opaque, prefaces that he composed for the New York Edition of his novels, James worked away at his central message to novelists present and future. It was, in Allen Tate's words, "Don't state . . . render! Don't tell us what is happening, let it happen!"[2] The novel, James kept insisting with the fineness of critical discernment and intensity of commitment to his chosen task characteristic of his genius, is nothing if not made palpable and complete. "The dramatist," he declared in his preface to *The Awkward Age*, "has verily to *build*, is committed to architecture, to construction at any cost; to driving in deep his vertical supports and laying across and firmly fixing his horizontal, his resting pieces—at the risk of no matter what vibration from the tap of his master-hammer."[3]

1. T. S. Eliot, from "Henry James," in Louis D. Rubin, Jr., and John Rees Moore eds., *The Idea of an American Novel* (New York, 1961), p. 246.

2. Allen Tate, "Techniques of Fiction," in *On the Limits of Poetry* (New York, 1948), p. 140.

3. Henry James, "Preface to *The Awkward Age*," in R. P. Blackmur ed., *The Art of the Novel*, Scribner Library ed. (New York, 1934), p. 109.

James's devotion to the art of fiction attained, more so even than Gustave Flaubert's and quite in keeping with the prevailing attitude toward art of the late nineteenth and the twentieth centuries, an almost religious character. Frequently he refers, in terms of affection and deep respect, to his "blessed old genius," the faculty of imagination that enabled him to perform his novelistic office. Try to be one of the people, he urged the young novelist, on whom nothing is lost; for James the novelist's vocation was nothing less than priestly, since it afforded him what no other vocation, however respected, could grant: the keenest possible insight into reality.

He insisted that the novel must explore consciousness; "the power to be finely aware and richly responsible," he declared, makes for interest and importance. "We care, our curiosity and our sympathy care, comparatively little for what happens to the stupid, the coarse and the blind," he asserts; "care for it, and for the effects of it, at the most as helping to precipitate what happens to the more deeply wondering, to the really sentient." [4] Neither the priest nor the philosopher might approach this ultimate privilege of the novelist's. Fully as deeply as Proust or Joyce did James believe that it was this power of the artist, and of the artist alone, that ultimately gave meaning to human consciousness. The novelist who could explore, uncover, "render" experience into an objectified image, who through technique could recreate the nature of reality, was the ultimate seer. He created; he "did." "Our noted behavior at large may show for ragged, because it perpetually escapes our control," he decided; "we have again and again to consent to its appearing in undress—that is in no state to brook criticism. But on all the

4. Henry James, "Preface to *The Princess Casamassima*," in *The Art of the Novel*, p. 62.

ground to which the pretension of performance by a series of exquisite laws may apply there reigns one sovereign truth—which
decrees that, as art is nothing if not exemplary, care nothing
if not active, finish nothing if not consistent, the proved error
is the base apologetic deed, the helpless regret is the barren commentary, and 'connections' are employable for finer purposes
than mere gaping contrition." [5] The famous dictum of Proust's,
that "in art excuses count for nothing; good intentions are of
no avail; the artist must at every moment heed his instinct;
so that art is the most real of all things, the sternest school
in life, and truly the Last Judgment," [6] claims no more than
James did for the office of the novelist.

Vital to this high estimate of the artist's role and function
was that the work of art thus created should exist, finally alone
—should be "rendered." For since the novel fulfills itself not
in the service of any higher and extraliterary truth, but *as itself*, with the purpose being one of achieving full consciousness,
of "knowing," the novel—James's chosen art form—can justify
itself only through the utmost realization of its own inherent
properties, its own form. This of course James referred right
back to the sensibility of the novelist; it is the responsibility
of the artist to know and to develop the meaning of his novel.
But that meaning, he insisted always, was to be pronounced not
outside of or parenthetical to his story, but within the story, and
as the story. What the artist knew, he knew as fiction, and the
process of acquiring knowledge was the process of creating fiction. "Correspondences!" he exhorted his fellow craftsmen; to
glimpse in a situation the possibilities for its expansion, to ex-

5. Henry James, "Preface to *The Golden Bowl*," in *The Art of the Novel*, p. 348.
6. Marcel Proust, *Remembrance of Things Past*, II (New York, 1932), p. 1001.

plore these possibilities within the situation until the novel had fully worked them out, so that coincidence became causality, resemblance became relationship, curiosity became motivation, and the dramatized scene became the revealed meaning—this was both the novelist's responsibility and his opportunity. "Dramatize, dramatize!" he told himself; it was his way of saying "understand, understand!"

James's belief in the supreme necessity for "rendering"—creating the scene fully—was thus his way of insisting that the novelist must work to understand and give order to his subject to the utmost limits of his capacity. Unfortunately his dictum has been fastened upon by some of James's followers and made to serve a very different purpose. By "dramatize!" James meant "reveal!" for to him this was the way the novelist went about understanding; but for others, the injunction to "dramatize!" has been made to mean "restrict yourself!" The Jamesian position, as interpreted by persons of narrower imagination and lesser sympathies, has come to mean that the novelist must pretend that he is writing a play, differing from formal drama only in that the novelist, unlike the playwright, can show his characters thinking as well as speaking and acting.

A great deal of polemical energy has been expended both by proponents of this theory of fiction and by those who oppose it, and precious little understanding of James's beloved art of fiction has been communicated in the process. Why the Jamesian theory should have touched off this passionate a debate is puzzling. Various questions enter into the so-called Question of Henry James, of course, having to do with the Anglophilia, his preference for "cultivated" characters instead of "men of action," the rival claims of "art" and "truth," his alleged snobbery, and so on. He is a hero to a Ford Madox Ford, a villain to a Maxwell Geismar—and it is difficult to read the polemics of either writer without being irresistibly attracted to the other side. I suspect that at the root of the controversy over Jamesian technique is a kind of polarity of temperament between those who prefer art as the process of discrimination and those whose preference is for art as augmentation. If this is true, the Jamesian mode would appear to be pre-eminently that of the exploration of discriminations, until what is given has been fully and finally discriminated. When at the end of *The Ambassadors* Lewis Lambert Strether announces to his friend Maria Gostrey, "Then there we are!", a puzzling social situation, beginning in obscurity and confusion and moving through complexity toward full understanding, has been worked out, and all has been understood. Our fascination is with the finer and finer discrimination which takes place as Strether masters his situation. It is right that Strether decides to make no selfish use of it for his own advantage, for to do so would sully the pure realization of what it has all been shown to mean. Those who dislike the Jamesian novel find such a process tiresome and trivial; their preference is for the novel which, from a given situation, proceeds not inward but outward, to possess more and more experience. This reader, if he is a critic, is likely to declare that the James novel lacks "life," by which he means the sense of the individual's being confronted by a more various and demanding experience than can be isolated and mastered through being explored in every one of its parts. He wants his fictional character to respond to experience by feeling one way or the other about it, not by a compulsion to possess the experience through analysis. Maxwell Geismar is an unhappy example of this kind of critic; at bottom he doesn't care what a novelist chooses to make out of this or that particular experience. He judges novelists by the social and political issues they are for or against.

A common mistake of the critic who dislikes James is to claim that he is essentially a passionless novelist; he is supposedly not interested in emotion, but in cold, cerebral analysis. He wants only to see how a situation is worked out, and not whether it is good or bad, whether one ought to like or dislike what is being analyzed. To anyone who enjoys Henry James no charge could be more absurd. There is no more passionate novelist alive or dead. His passion, however, was not for impulsive emotional response to something; it was for full understanding of it. He wanted to go beneath the surface, to penetrate the façade, and to find out what lay hidden beneath and beyond the obvious. The James novel typically begins where most novels leave off. What does a situation, a relationship between human beings, mean? He refused to content himself with the crudeness of immediate, obvious emotion; he would experience passion thoroughly through mastering its full meaning. As a younger and less obsessed Ezra Pound once declared of him, "The outbursts in *The Tragic Muse,* the whole of *The Turn of the Screw,* human liberty, personal liberty, the rights of the individual against all sorts of intangible bondage! The passion of it, the continual passion of it in this man who, fools said, didn't 'feel.' " [7]

On the other hand, the professional Jamesians are by no means without fault in this matter of "discrimination" versus "augmentation." Too often they tend to use James's preference for the full working out of a situation as a weapon to defend a literature that is not so much finely discriminated as simply neat and tidy. James's admonition to seek "correspondences!" is made into a sanction for fiction in which nothing is attempted that cannot be handily fitted into a scheme. James's desire for a "central intelligence" who can realize the full implications of

7. Ezra Pound, from "Henry James," in Rubin and Moore eds., *The Idea of an American Novel,* p. 243.

a situation is made to seem the assertion of a smug superiority over anyone incapable of the contemplative appreciation of trivia. And James's famous preference for the rendered, the dramatized scene, becomes a rigid, formula-ridden notion of fiction as being little more than a game of charades with dialogue.

That James, whose great inventiveness and receptivity to differing ways of writing are so much a part of his personality, should be made into an apologist for the tidy and the conventional in literature is surely a distressful business. Yet again and again one finds him being used in this manner. Where for James the passion for "discrimination" was a passion for the most thorough possible exploration, the ultimate savoring of an experience, he is made to appear as having a hostility to anything out of the ordinary. But James had the kind of mind which kept extending its bounds, though never at the expense of fully possessing what it took in. He was continually able, as a reader, to take advantage of what an author had to offer: Henry James was not the kind of person who let himself be shut off from literary experience by too rigid theoretical considerations. Again and again, as one reads his critical writings, one is struck by the generosity of his taste, and also by how much broader and more catholic his own sympathies are than those of many who profess to adhere to his standards.

Caroline Gordon, for example, in a book entitled *How to Read a Novel*, discusses the eighteenth-century novelists Richardson and Fielding. Richardson, she says, "lays the groundwork for the triumphs of Henry James" as well as for James Joyce's use of the stream of consciousness, because "by placing himself at the very center of vision—that is, within the consciousness of his heroine" he "achieves the immediacy which is the goal of every serious novelist." Fielding, on the other hand, stays at a distance; and as for his famous chapters of commentary, while "some learned and acute critics have argued that the 'reflective' chapters which he interspersed the narrative of *Tom Jones* actually constitute another 'plane of action,' " Miss Gordon has little use for the method. She scolds Robert Penn Warren for using the phrase "the novel of discourse" to cover these matters.[8]

How different this characteristically "Jamesian" reaction to Fielding's apparent failure to dramatize his scenes is from Henry James's own comment on Fielding's technique in his preface to *The Princess Casamassima*. Here is James himself on the character of Tom Jones:

He has so much "life" that it amounts, for the effect of comedy and application of satire, almost to his having a mind, that is to his having reactions and a full consciousness; besides which his author—*he* handsomely possessed of a mind—has such an amplitude of reflection for him and round him that we see him through the mellow air of Fielding's fine old moralism, fine old humor and fine old style, which somehow really enlarge, make every one and every thing important.[9]

While recognizing Fielding's failure to give his character the kind of consciousness that he might himself prefer for his own people, James refuses to let this objection inhibit his enjoyment of *Tom Jones*, and happily accepts Fielding's way of giving meaning to his novel. Not for nothing did Henry James consider himself a pragmatist like his brother William. *Tom Jones* obviously "worked"; James therefore didn't quibble very much over how its author managed it.

I have gone into James's personality and his temperament at some length, because I want to try to show how very much a part of his fiction that personality is. The idea that Henry James, of all people, practiced the art of fiction as if the personality of the novelist were not part of it, as if novels were not to appear

8. Caroline Gordon, *How to Read a Novel* (New York, 1957), p. 81.
9. "Preface to *The Princess Casamassima*," p. 68.

to be "written," has always seemed incredible to me. James not "in" his novels? No novelist who ever wrote is more "in" his novels than Henry James! His personality pervades every paragraph he wrote, and the delight and enjoyment of one's encounter with that personality is the hallmark of his fiction.

Consider *The Ambassadors*. Dramatized it is, and the scenic principle is definitely at work—one seldom encounters in fiction so rich and so fascinating a sequence of dramatic scenes. But to say, as Caroline Gordon does, that "James never appears on his scene," and that "his stories are not told; they are acted out as if on a stage," [10] is to attempt to elevate a skillful technical device into a rigid principle of esthetics. In the first place, James as himself *does* tell us a great deal during the course of *The Ambassadors;* whenever he wishes us to know how Lambert Strether will later interpret something currently happening to him, he steps in to inform us of this. When Chad Newsome first puts in an appearance while Strether and Marcia Gostrey are at the theatre, James considers it important for us to realize that Strether's first impression of Chad is going to remain with him for some time to come. So the author "intrudes" and addresses the reader directly:

Our friend [that is, James's and the reader's friend] was to go over it afterwards again and again—he was going over it much of the time that they were together, and they were together constantly for three or four days: the note had been so strongly struck during that first half-hour that everything happening since was comparatively a minor development.[11]

(James is constantly referring to Strether as "our friend"; which indeed he soon becomes.)

10. Gordon, pp. 117, 124.
11. Henry James, *The Ambassadors,* ed. S. P. Rosenbaum, Norton Critical ed. (New York, 1964), p. 89.

An instance early in *The Ambassadors* of James's telling us something he wants us to know but can't or won't permit the character to relate is the famous business about the supposedly "unmentionable" vulgar domestic item, the manufacture of which has made the Newsome fortune. Maria Gostrey is curious about what this item might be; Strether promises to tell her.

But [says James] it may even now frankly be mentioned that he, in the sequel, never was to tell her. He actually never did so, and it moreover oddly occurred that, by the law, within her, of the incalculable, her desire for the information dropped, and her attitude to the question converted itself into a positive cultivation of ignorance. In ignorance she could humour her fancy, and that proved a useful freedom. She could treat the little nameless object as indeed un-nameable —she could make their abstention enormously definite. There might indeed have been for Strether the portent of this in what she next said.[12]

That is not Strether speaking; it is Henry James, and he does so not only because he wants to inform us that he is never going to reveal what the Newsomes of Woollett, Massachusetts, manufacture, but also because he wants to sketch in the kind of person Maria Gostrey is, when it would be inappropriate for Lambert Strether to be able to do so at that stage of the story.

But such overt authorial "intrusion" is only one of the ways whereby the authorial personality of Henry James is part of our experience in reading *The Ambassadors*. Consider, for example, the matter of how much we know about what Strether is thinking, and when it is that we find out. Not until well into the narrative, in fact, do we learn *why* Strether is in Europe. Miss Gordon declares that James's "people reveal themselves to us gradually—the way people reveal themselves to us in life." [13] She sees this as a method of gaining "verisimilitude." But if

12. *The Ambassadors*, p. 48.
13. Gordon, p. 124.

"verisimilitude" means having the appearance of being "real," then that is precisely what the withholding of the facts of Strether's mission is *not*. Were Strether a lesser character whose function it is to be revealed through what the character of central intelligence learns about him, then the withholding of these things might be "the way people reveal themselves in life." But since we are inside Lambert Strether's mind from the beginning of the novel, and we share his thoughts, it is inconceivable, from a point of view of strict fidelity to "real life," that Strether would not have thought, many times before he finally begins talking about it to his friends Waymarsh and Maria Gostrey, of his mission and of those who have sent him on it.

The reason why these facts about Strether's mission are withheld for a time is that Henry James quite properly wants to build up suspense, to draw us further into Strether's situation so that we want to know more about it. James wants *us* to "discover" Strether; if he were to have Strether blurt out the facts of what he is thinking about his mission at the very start, on the grounds of "verisimilitude," he would have to sacrifice the delightful puzzlement of Strether's uneasiness, his hesitation, his enjoyment in feeling "reckless" because he is on the other side of the ocean from Woollett, Massachusetts, and so on.

In short, to be told part of what a character is thinking, but not all, not even all that is relevant, is not a device of "verisimilitude," and it is certainly no way to trick the reader into forgetting he is reading a novel, that he is being told a story. Rather, it is very much a convention of fiction, and we accept the convention only because we know that we are being told a a story. The principle of dramatization, of the scenic construction, operates *within that essential story-telling form*, and because it does, it becomes a part of our experience of being told the story. It becomes part, that is, of our experience of and relationship with the authorial personality, Henry James.

To attempt, therefore, to understand *The Ambassadors* without taking into account how much of the story's wonderful charm and suspense depend upon our consciousness of the authorial personality revealing it to us is to leave out much of the book's attraction for us. Who, after all, but Henry James could present for our delectation some of those marvelously oblique "dialogues" such as Strether and Maria Gostrey engage in? Surely they are not "realistic," in the sense that we know people who actually talk that way. Consider this extended bit of conversation:

"It's a plot," he declared—"there's more in it than meets the eye." He gave the rein to his fancy. "It's a plant!"

His fancy seemed to please her. "Whose then?"

"Well, the party responsible is, I suppose, the fate that waits for one, the dark doom that rides. What I mean is that with such elements one can't count. I've but my poor individual, my modest human means. It isn't playing the game to turn on the uncanny. All one's energy goes to facing it, to tracking it. One wants, confound it, don't you see?" he confessed with a queer face—"one wants to enjoy anything so rare. Call it then life"—he puzzled it out—"call it poor dear old life simply that springs the surprise. Nothing alters the fact that the surprise is paralyzing, or at any rate engrossing—all, practically, hang it, that one sees, that one *can* see."

Her silences were never barren, nor even dull. "Is that what you've written home?"

He tossed it off. "Oh dear, yes!"

She had another pause while, across her carpets, he had another walk. "If you don't look out you'll have them straight over."

"Oh but I've said he'll go back."

"And *will* he?" Miss Gostrey asked.

The special tone of it made him, pulling up, look at her long. "What's that but just the question I've spent treasures of patience and ingenuity in giving *you*, by the sight of him—after everything has led up—every facility to answer? What is it but just the thing I came here to-day to get out of you? Will he?"

"No—he won't," she said at last. "He's not free."

The air of it held him. "Then you've all the while known—?"

"I've known nothing but what I've seen; and I wonder," she declared with some impatience, "that you didn't see as much. It was enough to be with him there—"

"In the box? Yes," he rather blankly urged.

"Well—to feel sure."

"Sure of what?"

She got up from her chair, at this, with a nearer approach than she had ever yet shown to dismay at his dimness. She even, fairly pausing for it, spoke with a shade of pity. "Guess!" [14]

Nowhere except in the novels of Henry James do people converse in this fashion. The dialogue is about as far as one can get from the clumsiness, the approximations, of ordinary conversation—whether of the nineteenth or twentieth century does not matter. James himself, if we are to believe his friends, did indeed talk something like this, though with more hesitations and greater groping for the exact word. But that is just the point; the impress of the powerful personality of Henry James is stamped on every line of Lambert Strether's and Maria Gostrey's tête-a-têtes. It isn't that, like Confederate generals and Victorian heroines, his people talk in complete sentences. More importantly, the nuances, the stresses, the lovely precision of the interruptions give to their conversations an utterly original charm; James's people seem to exist in order to talk to each other. One would never think to apply ordinary standards of realistic reportage to a James conversation, for so-called "verisimilitude" is not involved. Nor should one fail to note that, however brilliant the characters' speech, it is by no means the only ingredient at work; James is constantly modulating, com-

14. *The Ambassadors*, pp. 105–06.

menting, stepping in to tell us precisely how to "hear" what is being said. It is no effaced author who informs us that Miss Gostrey is rather pleased by Strether's fancy, or that her "silences were never barren, nor ever dull." And what novelist besides Henry James could make even the silences between sentences of a conversation bear part of his meaning?

Not long after *The Ambassadors* was first published, James wrote to a friend that a copy of the novel was being sent to him. "Don't write to 'thank' me for it—," he declared, "but if you are able successfully to struggle with it try to like the poor old hero, in whom you will perhaps find a vague resemblance (though not facial!) to yours always HENRY JAMES." [15] Lewis Lambert Strether, of course, is not the biographical Henry James, any more than he is William Dean Howells, whose reported outburst to Jonathan Sturges furnished the germ about which James built his novel. (I am not sure, however, that there is not a great deal of Howells, as James saw him, in Strether's characterization.) Nevertheless, a powerful sense of sympathetic identification exists between James and his character, lying not only in the fondness with which this character is made to embody aspects of the personality of his creator, but also in the manner James uses to tell us what Strether is thinking. It is as if the true location, in the story, of the central intelligence is not in the scenes and events themselves, but in the central intelligence *as it thinks back on all that has happened*. In other words, one has the sense of the whole novel being recapitulated, and of its being composed as the act of that remembrance. And this despite the fact that each scene is indeed dramatized for us, in James's best manner.

This is probably going a bit too far; *The Ambassadors* is

15. Henry James, Letter, "To Jocelyn Persse," in *The Ambassadors*, p. 408.

surely not a "Remembrance of Things Past." What is more likely true is that one has a feeling throughout, as in all of James's later fiction, of the author's personality shaping and presenting the story, of the story's being, in short, "told" to us, or at any rate, "written" for us. We are very conscious of the authority on which we are being told things, and the authority is that of the author. We "take it" on his say-so, and our delight in so doing comes from his personality. To echo James on Fielding, we do indeed see Strether "through the mellow air of Henry James's fine old moralism, fine old humor and fine old style, which somehow really enlarge, make every one and every thing important!"

If we accept the role of that authorial personality—and remember, once again, that it is a *formal* property of the novel— we can perhaps better see the Jamesian insistence on the scenic, dramatic method for what it is: not a statement on the nature of fictional form, but a statement about technique. When James says that the novelist must render, must "dramatize, dramatize!", he is not confusing the novel with the theater, as some of his followers have done. He is urging that the novelist, within the given nature of fiction as a language art in which author and reader participate in an act of communication, do his utmost to make his story visible, alive, and believable. Far from demanding that the novelist create a game of charades with dialogue, as one might think if one read only Jamesians and not James himself, he would have his novelist bend every effort to tell a story as richly and as meaningfully as possible, and to overlook no possibility to tell his story more effectively. James was no man to attempt to evade his responsibility, to pretend to a lack of authority. It was "the mere muffled majesty of irresponsible 'authorship' " [16] that he abhorred; he would have his novelist

16. "Preface to *The Golden Bowl*," p. 328.

stand fully responsible for what he did, and James's objection to "authorial intrusion" was that it permitted a novelist to declare something was true without having to make his statement valid by creating it in his fiction. But as we have seen, in *The Ambassadors* James is himself a frequent "intruder." The difference is that when James "intruded," when he told us what Strether was thinking or would be thinking, he did not do so in order to evade having to create Strether's characterization properly, but in order to do what Strether could himself never do: be in two chronological positions simultaneously.

The Jamesian "scene design," then, is a method of technique, and those who take it as a principle of esthetics, and who believe that James thought the presence of the story teller in the reader's consciousness was a betrayal of the novelist's art, convert an essentially pragmatic attitude toward story telling into a rigid ideological position. For James the novel itself, the success of the fiction, was the single end of the novelist's craft. When the technique of dramatization, for all its great advantages in revealing a situation, got in the way of the reader's being told what he needed to know, James did not scruple to violate it.

The preoccupation with technique in critical writings about James, the fervor with which his admirers keep setting forth the Jamesian insistence upon dramatization, has always seemed to me to be a kind of tribute, however unwitting, to the role of the authorial personality of the James novels. I am impressed by the frequency with which these commentators talk about what James is "doing." There is nothing improper in this whatever, of course; but it does seem to indicate the extent to which, in a supposedly "rendered" novel by an impersonal author, the reader is conscious of the presence of the author. Can we really watch old Strether as he thinks and feels his way ever more deeply into the situation at hand, without constantly being aware—and to our continuing delight—of the hand of the Master as he arranges all this for us? And is not *The Ambassadors* ultimately *not* so much a novel of situation, however much James may have developed it in that sense, as a novel of character—the character being "our friend," whom we come fully to understand at last, existing in a highly dynamic relationship to the authorial personality who has presented him to us? What after all is the "goal" of the novel, if not to make Strether into "one of the people on whom nothing is lost"?—which is precisely the faculty James would have a novelist possess. Strether will write no novels; but as anyone knows who has read the entry in James's notebooks in which he concerns himself with the sort of person Strether should be, James in effect decides he must make him as close to being a novelist as possible without actually being one.[17] It is not, to repeat, that Strether is "autobiographical," in the sense that James is writing about his own life, but there is a great deal of Henry James in him; and no reader of *The Ambassadors* can fail to be caught up in the exhilaration involved in the telling of Strether by the author, a narration which is simultaneously a process of discovery.

Though I have confined this discussion of the authorial personality in James to *The Ambassadors,* almost any of his later work would have done almost as well to illustrate the manner in which the Jamesian personality is made central to the reader's experience. So apparently "external" and, Oscar Cargill on the sad case of Alice James to the contrary, so "unautobiographical" a novella as the famous *The Turn of the Screw* is equally imbued with the presence of the authorial personality, even though the story, except for the introductory chapter, is a first-person

17. Henry James, Notebook Entry, quoted in *The Ambassadors*, p. 373.

affair narrated by the Governess, who is certainly not Henry
James. What happens in *The Turn of the Screw?* It has been
written about exhaustively. There can be little doubt that the
Governess' own story is wildly inconsistent; again and again
she can be detected in lies, in exaggerations, in reporting scenes
she did not see and conversations that did not take place, in
making inferences that are unjustified by facts. All that we
know about the famed season at Bly is her account; but she did
not know how to conceal what she had to conceal if we were
to believe her. And if all that were not enough, James opens
his story with a little preface telling how the Governess narrative was read to a group of his friends by an elderly gentleman
named Douglas. Examined closely, Douglas' own explanation
of his relationship to the manuscript and the Governess shows
up as not without its mystery; there is the definite hint that
Douglas may even be the little boy Miles in the narrative, whom
the Governess had supposedly frightened to death! [18] But if that
is true, then what is the Governess narrative but sheer fantasy,
and where does it leave us? It leaves us with Henry James, who
with consummate artistry has led us off in one direction after another, with the trail constantly doubling back on itself, so that
we are confronted finally with the personality of the author.
What *did* he intend to do? I am convinced that the only answer
to this question is that he schemed to present a conundrum, and
that he did so splendidly. The careful reader's response to *The
Turn of the Screw*, I think, is immediately to try to figure out
what the author was trying to do, and this is precisely what

---

18. My feeling that this is James's intention is quite strong, notwithstanding that so eminent an authority on James as Mr. Leon Edel has dismissed it
as utterly without merit [letter to author]. My own essay setting forth this
theory, among others, is "One More Turn of the Screw," *Modern Fiction
Studies,* IX, 4 [Winter 1963–64], 314–328.

James wanted. If anyone doubts that Henry James knew what was involved in this stratagem, he need only read his remarks on Joseph Conrad's *Chance*, in which he explains how Conrad's use of Marlow as a narrator finally throws the reader back on the personality of Conrad himself, to the reader's infinite enjoyment.[19]

There are those who would insist that all this kind of thing is "extraliterary," "biographical," and so on. In what way, I cannot understand. To savor fully the rich personality of the person telling us a story, to become enthralled in the story he is telling because of the way in which he tells it—surely this is part of one's formal experience of a novel. Especially with the fiction of Henry James, any theory of reading novels, any critical analysis of those novels, which leaves out the pleasure involved in the rendered personality of the author himself, must constitute needless impoverishment. Always present, always at our right arm as we read, never so artful and so enjoyably sly as when he pretends to be giving us only "straight facts," he is without equal in what he does. There may be other methods of telling a story than James's—he reminds us that the house of fiction contains many, many windows—but none more suited to the man himself. He found *his* way—so deftly that one would scarcely want Henry James to be anything more or other than what he abundantly is.

19. Henry James, "The New Novel," in *The Future of the Novel*, ed. Leon Edel, Vintage ed. (New York, 1956), pp. 279–84.

FIVE · The Self Recaptured

THERE is a certain attitude toward literature that treats
Henry James and Marcel Proust as if they were essentially
the same kind of novelist. The linkage of the two names is
usually preceded by the disclaimer, however camouflaged, "I
don't go for. . . ." Both James and Proust are novelists of
society, they spend long chapters chronicling the happenings in
drawing rooms, so therefore they are that variety of novelist—
just as Theodore Dreiser, James T. Farrell, Ernest Hemingway,
and John Dos Passos are a different variety, because they do not
customarily concern themselves with drawing rooms. The basis
of this sort of criticism is obviously social: it arises out of a
prejudice against novelists of caste and class. It can also be political; novelists who concern themselves with the idle rich, who
prefer Madame de Vionnet and the Duc de Guermantes to Studs
Lonigan or Clyde Griffiths, are obviously kindred antidemocratic snobs (at this point mention of Hemingway's famous
retort to Fitzgerald—"the very rich are somehow different from
us"—"yeah, they've got more money"— is appropriate). Or—
a different kind of critical response—James and Proust are alike
because each one indulges in long, exhaustive descriptions of the
conversations at dinner parties and the like, instead of dealing
with more important things. This attitude is not necessarily
political, or even social; it comes closer to being psychological,
having to do with the reader's temperament. But all too often,
I think, its assertion is a confession of laziness, having to do with

the fact that to appreciate James or Proust one must be willing to take fiction seriously enough to read them closely and carefully. One can, for example, read *Moby-Dick* casually, and still enjoy the account of a fine whaling expedition, even though missing most of the meaning of the characterization of Captain Ahab; or one can read "The Nigger of the Narcissus" in the same way that one reads, say, Joshua Slocum's *Sailing Alone Around the World*. Try reading *The Wings of the Dove* or *Within a Budding Grove* that way; very little is likely to be of interest.

James and Proust do have their affinities, of course; each focused his art on the social relationship; and since the relationship of people to each other involved and involves manners and status, each one commonly chose for the objects of his examination persons whose everyday relationships most dramatically and, as it were, directly focused upon these problems. Is this antidemocratic snobbishness? One might reply, as Marius Bewley does, that such charges as brought against James

boil down to some such elementary proposition as this: he imagined that, other things being equal, a man or woman might achieve a more sensitive degree of awareness, a finer quality of mind and heart, if he lived among people and surroundings of taste than if he lived on a chicken farm in South Dakota or in a cold water flat on Rutgers Street.[1]

Of course with Proust it goes further even than that; Proust as a novelist (and as a man) was interested in snobbery, was not unsympathetic to it in some of its aspects, and yet the ultimate result was one of the most penetrating and even savage dissections of snobbery and caste ever composed. To dissect

1. Marius Bewley, *The Eccentric Design: Form in the Classic American Novel* (New York, 1959), p. 250.

something well, one must understand it, and in order to understand something one must have a certain amount of sympathy with it; but does this argument make, say, William Faulkner into a racist, or Stendhal into an ultra-royalist?

The so-called similarity between James and Proust, to conclude, is principally one of a common subject matter; and while the resemblance might be worthy of consideration in a study of the novel in terms of social and political documentation, it has little relevance beyond that. As for other similarities, which *do* have relevance beyond that of subject matter, these are less often mentioned, and not surprisingly, for they comport but poorly with any argument preceded by the words "I don't go for. . . ." They have to do with a common belief in the role of art as the ultimate exploration of life, a common impatience with superficial judgments, a common belief in the need for the novelist to develop to the fullest possible extent of consciousness the implications and relationships of a situation. They have to do, that is, with a kindred conviction that "in art, excuses count for nothing," and that the novelist must by the nature of his vocation be "one of those on whom nothing is ever lost." Neither James nor Proust placed his muse at the service of mere expediency. Neither chose to oversimplify for the sake of easy communication. For both, the chief enemy was superficiality.

One might appropriately sum up the whole matter by saying that both James and Proust were stylists. This is more than simply saying that both writers used language in ways characteristically and identifiably their own. Both of them used an elaborate, complex, "written" style, one that included rather than excluded, that encompassed complex experience and made it into a unit, balanced nuances and shades of meaning, searched out relationships and explored analogies: richly transformed, that is, the documentation of life into the order and form of art. James's exhortation to his fellow writers, to seek "correspondences! Correspondences!", is of the same nature as Proust's famous dictum that

truth will begin only when the writer takes two different objects, establishes their relationship—analogous in the world of art to the sole relationship in the world of science, the law of cause and effect—and encloses them in the necessary rings of a beautiful style. . . . (II, 1008)[2]

For James as for Proust language must reach out and assimilate what it seeks to describe, envelop it in balance and meaning; and so both writers wrote long and involved sentences in order to portray the world as they saw it. Needless to say, with Proust as well as James one result is the establishment of a profound consciousness, on the part of the reader, of the author's presence and personality. One doesn't, after all, speak first of *The Ambassadors*, of *Remembrance of Things Past*; one speaks of James, of Proust; for there are few novelists whose work is so idiosyncratic, so much the embodiment of a special personality.

I have gone into this matter at some length principally because, if a certain type of reader is prone to link James and Proust together for the wrong reasons, there is another, and I think generally much more responsible, kind of critic who is likely to think of the two writers as being antipodal, as representing almost diametrically opposite approaches to the writing of fiction. Unlike silly prejudices about snobbery and political attitudes, there is a great deal to be said for this position. It is, that James is pre-eminently the dramatizer, the writer of scenes, for whom his own personal experience is but the merest

2. Marcel Proust, *Remembrance of Things Past*, 2 vols., trans. C. K. Scott Moncrieff and Frederick A. Blossom (New York, 1932). All quotations from the book are taken from this edition, and are given parenthetically.

donnée, the germ from which his fiction is developed; while Proust, despite his brilliance at depicting certain great scenes, is just as pre-eminently the nondramatic, autobiographical novelist, whose work is proudly and profoundly taken from his own experience.

The writings of each about the art of fiction tend abundantly to confirm this distinction. We know, from James's prefaces and from the evidence of his notebooks, what he thought about the process whereby life is made into art. An overheard conversation, a remark by a friend, an incident reported to him, strikes fire in his imagination. Thereupon he begins thinking about it, meditating on its possible ramifications of meaning, invents characters in order to develop it, a plot to give it life and form, resulting first in a scenario whereby the dimensions of the novel are worked out, often at exhaustive length, and only finally in the novel itself. Nothing might seem further from Proust's way; with Proust the process was memory, the recapture of his own personal experience:

This book, the most difficult of all to discover, is also the only one dictated to us by reality, the only one the "imprinting" of which on our consciousness was done by reality itself. No matter what idea life may have implanted within us, its material representation, the outline of the impression it has made upon us, is always the guarantee of its indispensable truth. (II, 1001)

And,

I perceived that, to describe these impressions, to write that essential book, the only true book, a great writer does not need to invent it, in the current sense of the term, since it already exists in each of us, but merely to translate it. The duty and the task of a writer are those of translator. (II, 1009)

In the final analysis, of course, it makes no difference whether or not a novelist "invents" his material or whether he draws it directly from concrete experience, his own or others'. What matters is what he does with it, with how well he transforms it into fiction. If we grant this, then we are prepared to recognize a strong similarity between the processes whereby the Jamesian and the Proustian artistry evolve. For is not the celebrated madeleine episode in *Swann's Way*, so far as what happens in the writing of fiction is concerned, very much like the Jamesian habit of seizing upon the "germ" of a situation and then exploring it to the fullest possible realization of its meaning? From the Proustian donnée, the immediate, sensory memory, the novelist recaptures place and person, scene and meaning. Neither process will permit strict, immediate surface reportage; both involve extension, exploration, the expansion of detail which is also the giving of order and form.

The chief formal difference between the way of Henry James and that of Marcel Proust with a novel, then, is not that the former "evolves" a fiction from a "germ," while the latter does no more than borrow his in large chunks from his own life, giving to the raw material nothing but the ornamentation of a poetic style and changing a few things around for the sake of a better story.

Instead, the most striking difference would seem to be the technique by which the story is told. The James novels are "rendered" dramatically by the author; *Remembrance of Things Past* is told by a narrator who "remembers" what is described. That James's presence, as implied authorial personality, is strongly in evidence I have already sought to show; but that is another thing entirely from a novel which is not only told in the first person, but in which the first person narrator writes directly about himself when younger. Here, one might say, there is more than a merely apprehended personality telling us the story; the authorial personality is a definite individual, a character. He even calls himself by the real-life novelist's first name.

Not only that, but the narrator as well as the younger "I" about whom he writes evolves before our eyes during the course of the novel. The character Marcel grows up in Combray, meets Swann, falls in love with Gilberte, goes to Balbec with his grandmother where he meets Albertine, comes to know the Duchesse de Guermantes, the Baron Charlus, and the Verdurins, takes Albertine for a mistress and then loses her, goes away to a sanatorium and then returns to Paris during the First World War, and finally attends a party at the Prince de Guermantes where he recognizes his true vocation and prepares to write a novel. All this and more is told to us by the narrator, who as he goes along develops a series of hypotheses and general laws about human conduct, which are summed up and elaborated in the final episode in which he tells about himself as he came to recognize his true vocation. The narrator, in other words, describes how he came to write his novel, and the telling of it is the novel we read.

The discovery of the vocation involved the discovery as well of a method, which was at once a device of technique and a revelation of the nature of art and memory. The narrator stumbles momentarily upon two uneven paving stones as he alights from his carriage en route to the Guermantes soiree. He is overcome by a sensation of happiness. He resolves to grasp its cause and its meaning:

Each time that I merely repeated the action physically, the effort was in vain; but if I forgot the Guermantes reception and succeeded in recapturing the sensation I had felt the instant I placed my feet in that position, again the dazzling, elusive vision brushed me with its wings, as if to say, "Seize me in my flight, if you have the power, and try to solve the riddle of happiness I propound to you." And almost immediately I recognized it; it was Venice, about which my efforts at description and the supposed 'snapshots' taken by my memory had never yielded me anything, but which was brought back to me by the sensation I had once felt as I stood on two uneven flagstones in the baptistry of Saint Mark's, and with that sensation came all the others connected with it that day, which had been waiting in their proper place in the series of forgotten days, until a sudden happening had imperiously commanded them to come forth. (II, 992)

Out of this revelation, and the joy it inspired, the narrator realizes and tells us that the key to the redemption of his identity in time, and to the consummation of his career as writer, is the recreation through sensory memory of what he had known and been. He will rescue what he has been from the erosion of the years by fixing it permanently in art. All he has known and done up to that moment has been in the nature of a vocation, which has furnished him with the nourishment from which he will create the work of art that will give life order and meaning.

In the opening pages of the novel, we observe this process at work. The narrator relates a single episode about his family and himself, involving a party at which Charles Swann is present but from which he is barred, and in his room upstairs he sobs for his mother's presence until finally it is granted him. The episode, he tells us, is crucial to what he will become, but why it is crucial we do not yet understand. Then he informs us that this episode was for many years all that he remembered from his early childhood in Combray, until one day he had sat with his mother and had dipped a wafer into a cup of tea, whereupon the sensory memory thus occasioned reveals to him the universe of his childhood at Combray, in all its color, light, and concrete form.

At this juncture, we have not yet read *The Past Recaptured;*

we do not therefore know the importance of that process for the narrator. Its chief function seems to be only that it touched off the memory of Marcel at Combray that is described in the subsequent pages. Not until much later, at the end of the immensely long account of Marcel's life, do we realize that the process of rediscovery resulting in the unfolding of the Combray sequence was the key to the entire novel, and that what we have read existed only because the process was revealed for the narrator.

Needless to say, nothing in Henry James's fiction corresponds to this business. It is quite true that sometimes the author of *The Ambassadors* makes us aware, as we read the novel, that he knows the outcome of the story as he tells it, so that he can let us know what "our friend" Strether's response to an incident or piece of intelligence will later be. But the Jamesian story teller, the authorial personality, generally works through drammatized scenes alone, and he is almost never anything other than an authorial voice whose presence we sense and enjoy, often to the point of taking him entirely for granted. The narrator of Proust's novel, by contrast, constantly "intrudes" his presence by talking directly to us, making judgments, telling us what characters are thinking, anticipating and sometimes recalling as well, and often taking the center of the stage almost to the virtual exclusion of the younger Marcel he once was and whose life he describes. This narrator "develops" as he goes along; he knows a great deal more at the end than at the beginning, and he knows what it means, in part by virtue of retelling his life story. He is, in short, a discernible character in the novel.

Can he then be both a fictional character and also the authorial personality telling us his story?

With this question, we come to the heart of the matter of the way in which a certain kind of novel is told—the so-called "autobiographical novel." It is this kind of novel that is involved in any discussion of Marcel Proust's fiction, and I want now to discuss some of the problems of fictional form arising from the novel in which the author is apparently writing directly about his own life.

At the risk of belaboring the customary clichés involved in the matter, it might be wise at first to settle on a few principles. Obviously all fiction is "autobiographical," in the sense that the writer can know no other life than what he has experienced. When Thomas Wolfe, belatedly perturbed at the reception that *Look Homeward, Angel* might get in Asheville, prefixed a statement to his readers that "all serious work in fiction is autobiographical—that, for instance, a more autobiographical work than 'Gulliver's Travels' cannot easily be imagined," [3] he was attempting to slide by the problem. For undeniably there is fiction in which the events, people, and private concerns of the author's life are used directly and recognizably, and also fiction in which no direct and recognizable relationship seems to exist; it is the former variety that we term "autobiographical." Nobody ever wonders "who" Maria Gostrey was in real life; but as I write this, the identity of the Duchesse de Guermantes is the subject of a dispute in the letters columns of the *Times Literary Supplement* of London.[4] The distinction, I believe, is valid, and the assertion that there is such a kind of novel is defensible.

Yet just as obviously, attempts to deal with this matter biographically come up against the stern fact that it is all but im-

---

3. Thomas Wolfe, "To the Reader," *Look Homeward, Angel* (New York, 1929), p. vii.

4. See "Letters to the Editor," *Times Literary Supplement* (London), nos. 3311 (August 12, 1965), p. 697; 3312 (August 10, 1965), p. 715; 3313 (August 26, 1965), p. 735.

possible for the reader to know when a good novelist is transcribing his own experience directly and when he is "inventing." If, as I speculated in the previous chapter, there is a bit more of William Dean Howells in the makeup of Lewis Lambert Strether than Henry James affected to admit in his notes and preface to *The Ambassadors,* this is scarcely important either statistically or qualitatively to our experience of reading the novel. *The Ambassadors* simply isn't "that kind of novel," and neither, for example, is Scott Fitzgerald's *The Great Gatsby* "that kind of novel." The relationship of either to the lives of their authors is important thematically, but not in its page-by-page factual details. Could anyone, even a Freudian, get very far with James's *The Turn of the Screw* by attempting to work out the relationship of the specific events described to the biography of the author?

Compare that kind of relationship, or lack of it, with a novel such as Proust's, and the difference is unmistakable. We know of course that Proust drew upon his highly subjective memories of many people to make up his characters, and that there is no literal, one-for-one relationship involved. But just the same, we can work out some of the relationships, and the Proustian biographer, be he Richard Barker or George D. Painter, properly spends a great deal of his time pointing them out for us. Not only that, but the relationship *interests us;* to realize that, we have only to think of what our reactions would be upon viewing a photograph of Henry James's childhood governess as compared with what they would be upon seeing a photograph of the Proust family cook.

Is this merely because Proust has his narrator say that he is "remembering" Françoise, while James enters into no such dimension? Not at all, for the man named Douglas who is host in the house at which the ghost stories are being told, and who sends for and reads his old governess' narrative that constitutes the body of *The Turn of the Screw*, sets up just such a relationship; he too recalls his youth, and his friendship with the governess. And even if it were possible to imagine James having written a story much like *The Turn of the Screw* in which someone like Douglas, rather than the Governess, were the author of the narrative that follows, I doubt that we would be much more interested in tracking down the governess' real-life counterparts than we are. To repeat, it simply isn't "that kind of novel."

But *Remembrance of Things Past is* that kind of novel, and Marcel Proust certainly recognized this, as in that incredible moment in *The Captive* in which he has his narrator, referring to the death of Charles Swann, write as follows:

To a later generation, Cartier has become something so formless that it would be almost adding to his importance to make him out as related to the jeweller Cartier, with whom he would have smiled to think that anybody could be so ignorant as to confuse him! Swann on the contrary was a remarkable personality, in both the intellectual and the artistic worlds; and even although he had 'produced' nothing, still he had a chance of surviving a little longer. And yet, my dear Charles ——, whom I used to know when I was still so young and you were nearing your grave, it is because he whom you must have regarded as a little fool has made you the hero of one of his volumes that people are beginning to speak of you again and that your name will perhaps live. If in Tissot's picture representing the balcony of the Rue Royale club, where you figure with Galliffet, Edmond Polignac and Saint-Maurice, people are always drawing attention to yourself, it is because they know that there are some traces of you in the character of Swann. (II, 519)

Scott Moncrieff, in his translation, distorts Proust's point a little in inserting merely a dash after the name Charles, whereas Proust apparently wrote "Charles Swann,"[5] but the novelist knew quite well that many of his contemporary readers would be familiar with the Tissot portrait of Charles Haas and others that he cites, and would also long since have recognized some of Charles Haas's characteristics in Swann.[6] Proust was thus deliberately and amusingly pointing out for them the fact that he was composing "autobiographical" fiction, while also making a strong point in his developing thesis on the nature of art and time—and, it might be added, increasing our faith in the apparent "authority" of the narrator by a trick reminiscent of Cervantes' having his characters make allusions to the first volume of *Don Quixote* early in the course of the second volume.

Who "was" Charles Swann? Painter tells us he was composed out of the author's memories of Haas, Nicolas de Benardaky, Charles Ephrussi, Paul Hervieu, and Émile Straus, among others, and there is no reason to doubt this. Yet I would conjecture that had one been able to ask any number of long since dead French bon vivants this question, they would have replied without hesitation that Swann was this or that particular person, Haas or Benardaky or any one of the others, and would have also denied that there was anything important in the portrait of Swann that did not exist in his prototype. In other words—and I am sure that the authors of many other so-called "autobiographical" novels would verify this—there are novels in which not only are the characters and events recognizable to others besides the author, but that seem to demand biographical interpretation, to the extent that the author's "inventiveness" is scarcely credited at all. In part this can be laid

5. See the Pleiade ed., *A La Recherche du Temps Perdu*, III: *La Prissonnière* (Paris, 1954), p. 200.
6. George D. Painter, *Proust: The Early Years* (Boston, 1959), p. 116.

to poor readership; the reader who "knew" Charles Haas is a poor reader of Proust because he goes at the matter biographically and without making the proper imaginative response that will enable him to take part in the fictional relationship.

There is more to it than this, however. Often we read a novel by an unknown writer and we declare that it must surely be autobiographical. How do we know? Is it because real life has been but imperfectly transformed into art? Perhaps. But I doubt it. It seems to me that any reader encountering *Swann's Way* for the first time will have the feeling that the book is autobiographical, without thereby rendering an adverse critical judgment. This is not because of the presence of a narrator saying that he is remembering his past, either; countless first-person novels set up this relationship, and yet occasion no such response. Does anyone contend that *The Great Gatsby* must be a direct transcription of the actual events of Fitzgerald's life, merely because Nick Carraway talks about his past life and his encounter with Jay Gatsby? Furthermore, Proust did invent a great deal; there was, for example, apparently no Odette de Crécy in the life of Charles Haas.

When we speak of autobiographical fiction, we are not really discussing the personality of the biographical author and his relationship to the experience he writes about, but instead, identifying a *formal* relationship inherent in the fiction. This is a relationship created by the author (whether intentionally or not does not matter) and perceived by the reader (whether consciously or not does not matter, either). Not all novels drawn more or less directly out of the writer's specific experience have this relationship—apparently *The Sun Also Rises* contains a great deal of Hemingway's activities, but few would consider this of much importance. Not all novels involving a narrator talking about former times have it. Many novels which contain no reminiscing narrator embody this autobiographical relationship—*Look Homeward, Angel,* for one, or, as I shall attempt to show in a subsequent chapter, *A Portrait of the Artist as a Young Man* and *Ulysses*. And finally, the relationship could conceivably exist when there actually is no specific authorial experience involved at all.

If not necessarily between a first-person narrator and the past he discusses, then where is this relationship to be found? It exists, I think, between the events being described and the authorial personality telling the story, and who may or may not be the first-person narrator. It exists formally, in the way in which the story is told to us by the created, "implied author."

This implied author, the authorial personality whose presence is part of our experience of reading fiction, enters into a specific relationship with his material: that of memory and recall. He presents his subject matter in a way that makes us see that it is being drawn out of his own specific past, and that its being set forth involves his remembering it. The authorial personality not only tells us the story, but by making us aware that he is remembering what is going on and that it happened to him, he becomes in his own way a dramatized character.

This, to repeat, is often a far different matter from the first-person narrator saying that he remembers what he is telling us. Robert Penn Warren's novel *Band of Angels* opens, for example, with a situation very much like that in the opening pages of the *Remembrance of Things Past*. A first-person narrator begins with this statement: "Oh, who am I?," and then immediately adds, "For so long that was, you might say, the cry of my heart." [7] She thinks about her childhood, talks of her dreams of it, discusses her dead mother, describes her nurse, her father,

7. Robert Penn Warren, *Band of Angels* (New York, 1955), p. 3.

the life she lived. Yet I doubt that anyone would ever think that *Band of Angels* was autobiographical, and not merely or importantly because the narrator is feminine and the author a man (after all, certain male Proustian characters were no doubt female in real life!) Why not? Because while a relationship involving memory is set up between the first-person narrator and the events described, none is set up between the authorial personality telling the story of that narrator and those events she is made to remember, or between the first-person narrator and the authorial personality. The narrator is purely and solely a fictional character, who is remembering.

If we compare this with the opening of Proust's novel, we can see the difference at once. Proust's narrator likewise recalls his childhood and his dreams, and discusses the latter at some length. But whereas in Warren's novel we immediately have the feeling that the narrator is describing her childhood in order to set up the events that will soon change her life and launch her on her terrible ordeal, in Proust there is no comparable sense of anticipation, of a direction being established. Instead, almost as soon as the first-person narrator begins his discourse on sleep and awakening with the famous sentence, "For a long time I used to go to bed early," we are made to realize that Proust is out to do more than set up a psychological portrait of the "I" who is addressing us. By concentrating on the experience that the "I" is describing in a particular way, he makes clear that the act is a kind of ritual, and that it is being described not only for the sake of characterizing the first-person narrator, but in order to recreate the ritual. He says, "I *used to go* to bed early," "my eyes *would close* so quickly," "the thought that it was time to go to sleep *would awaken* me; I *would try* to put away the book. . . ." (I, 3) [Italics mine.] He is intent on showing us that the experience being described happened not once but often, and he concentrates on the luminous details of the experience, which is obviously out of the past, so that he draws us into the act of recapturing it. The experience of memory is thus absolutely necessary to the passage; it is the dominant mode of the fictional experience.

Whose memory can it be? Proust has made us focus our attention on the process of memory, not the meaning of it for the characterization of the first-person narrator. We thus become so conscious of the personality manipulating the first-person narrator, for whom the narrator is speaking, that the autobiographical relationship is set up. In other words, from the outset we must read *Remembrance of Things Past* not only for what is happening in the action (a first-person narrator talking about himself when a child), but for its relationship to the authorial personality. And as Proust often does, he actually tells us, in an oblique fashion, what he is doing, for he says of the book the child had been reading that "my thoughts had run into a channel of their own, until I myself seemed actually to have become the subject of my book. . . ." (I, 3) (Note the word *seemed*.) The dimension of memory is involved; again, not the first-person narrator's memory alone, but that of the authorial personality as he describes the narrator remembering. There are thus three different times involved: the childhood of Marcel, the adulthood of the remembering narrator, and the time at which the authorial personality is remembering and creating.

We might think of it this way. The dramatic tension set up in the opening pages of *Remembrance of Things Past* does not arise out of what the memories therein recounted mean about a fictional first-person narrator, as in *Band of Angels*. There is no comparable plot buildup. Instead, the excitement lies in the story teller's memories and what he thinks about them, for their own sake, and there is *no important separation,* at that juncture, between the author and the first-person narrator. They are one and the same, so far as we can tell, and in part this is the result of the extent to which the narrator goes on, speculating about the events he remembers without thereby leading us toward an action. Where Robert Penn Warren is interested in using his narrator's memories to set up a dramatic situation, Proust is concerned with the meaning of the memories themselves, and the reader is caught up in learning what the narrator says the memories, and the speculations they inspire, mean. Memory for its own sake is the matter on which our attention is focused. The narrator and the authorial personality are one and the same here, and the temporal dimension constitutes the "story." It is therefore, we say without hesitation, "autobiographical," for when the authorial personality goes about remembering things for their own sake, they are obviously his own. In other words, the authorial personality becomes the point of temporal focus upon which the meaning of the fiction centers, and the meaning lies in his memories. That is, purely and simply, what autobiographical fiction is.

Let me stress once again that I am talking about the formal structure of the novel, not the psychology of readership. The autobiographical dimension is *in* the novel, in the words, images, scenes, syntax. This dimension cannot be avoided; if the novel is read with any attention, it is inescapable. The reader may not consciously realize that this is going on, but he cannot help viewing the events of the novel from this perspective. And this, it seems to me, is why, in *Remembrance of Things Past,* the episode entitled "Swann in Love," though apparently a violation of the point of view because it involves material that Marcel himself could not really have known either when young or as narrator, nevertheless seems appropriate. The authorial personality, the remembering perspective from which we are seeing the action and whose relationship to the events is made part of our reading, can quite legitimately "possess," through his own deductive imagination, Swann's experience as well as Marcel's. Nor are we really disturbed when later in the novel some of Swann's experience tends to become Marcel's as well—the Vinteuil Sonata, for example, which means so much to Swann and later, through what process we are not sure, is made part of the adult Marcel's experience. This is surely a flaw in the logic of the point of view, which in another kind of novel would seriously spoil the form of the work, but which in Proust is not important. The created authorial personality being the dominant *persona* that it is in the novel, this seems a minor detail indeed. The mind of the authorial personality: that is what is most important.

Earlier I raised the question of whether the narrator of a novel can be both a fictional character and also the authorial personality telling us the story: his own story, that is. Obviously the answer is that he can be, as he is for much of Proust's novel, but also that he needn't be. The important thing is that the authorial personality of an autobiographical novel dramatizes his personality through its relation to the subject matter. Proust chose to do this by becoming, as it were, his narrator. I mean, of course, the authorial personality who is Proust, and not the biographical, real-life Marcel Proust who in certain interesting respects held different views and apparently had different tastes and habits from the authorial personality who tells the story.

In a different kind of autobiographical novel, there may be no narrator at all, or he may not be the spokesman for the authorial personality. The first-person narrator of Samuel Butler's *The Way of All Flesh*, for example, serves as a device through which the authorial personality can present the life and thoughts of Ernest Pontifex, who is the autobiographical character and whose experience the authorial personality is remembering. Ordinarily both these characters—the narrator and Ernest—are surrogates for Butler, but there are times when the first-person narrator turns to criticizing certain youthful enthusiasms of Ernest Pontifex of which the authorial personality doesn't really disapprove at all. When the child Ernest forwards a musical phrase from Handel to the narrator to set upon his aunt's gravestone, and tells the narrator that if it will not serve, he thinks he will use it for his own, the narrator affects to be disgusted with the youth's conceit. But the authorial personality is not, as we can tell from the way in which the episode is described.[8]

Thomas Wolfe's first novel, *Look Homeward, Angel*, has no formal narrator, except for the novelist's use of "I" in the early stages of the book before Eugene Gant is born. Yet a relationship of memory between the authorial personality and the central character is as palpable and as real as it is in Proust. When the novel opens, Eugene Gant is a long way from being born, and Wolfe is telling of how Eugene's father, W. O. Gant, came to Altamont from Pennsylvania. But Wolfe makes it very clear that the story is being *told to us* by the authorial personality—we don't at this point know for sure that the book to be autobiographical as well. He opens with a thematic commentary on time, destiny, and chance. He describes W. O. Gant's father's arrival in Pennsylvania, and after that Gant's boyhood. The editorial voice of the novelist is kept very much in the forefront: "But I know that [Gant's] cold and shallow eyes had darkened with the obscure and passionate hunger that had lived in a dead man's eyes, and that had led from Fenchurch Street past Phila-

8. Samuel Butler, *The Way of All Flesh*, World's Classics ed. (Oxford, n.d.), pp. 157–58.

delphia," he says at one point.[9] He relates Gant's journey from the piedmont town of Sydney to the mountain town of Altamont in great detail, and tells us what Gant is feeling and thinking. Then he describes the Pentland family into which Gant marries. Finally, after a vivid scene in which Gant, drunk, curses and reviles his wife, Eugene is born.

We get a commentary on the state of the world at the time of Eugene's birth, following which Wolfe describes and interprets Eugene's earliest thoughts, emotions, and experiences with the utmost care. The emphasis has thus been moved from the father to the child, where it will remain for most of the rest of the novel. And Wolfe soon adds another dimension; not only does he tell us what Eugene is thinking and feeling at the time, but he begins to inform us of what Eugene *later* came to think about all this, when older. Describing the activities at the house next door, for example, he says that

this ritual, followed closely from his father's sitting-room window, fascinated Eugene for years after: the people and the life next door were crudely and symbolically above him.[10]

During all this time Wolfe has been building up our sense of Eugene's consciousness, and the kind of thoughts and emotions Eugene has. Gradually we come to identify the authorial personality with that of Eugene when older; what is deemed important, both to the authorial personality and to Eugene, is inevitably what Eugene sees and thinks. We soon sense the same relationship of event and meaning that we have in Proust: what concerns the authorial personality is both the dramatic relevance of what is taking place to the development of Eugene's character, and the imaginative recreation of what took place for its

9. *Look Homeward, Angel*, p. 4.
10. *Ibid.*, p. 42.

own sake. There is the same luminous quality of ritual, of memory. Old Gant building a fire is characterization, but also recreation of a memory. The perspective has been thoroughly established; we are engaged in observing an authorial personality recreating the events of his childhood in order to understand them. It is an autobiographical novel.

There would appear to be little or nothing in an author's choice of actual events that he wishes to describe that makes a novel "autobiographical." The quality lies rather in the manner in which he describes them. I have called it a "luminous" quality; I mean by this that the event, the object, the incident, the memory is described in such a way that it seems to shine forth in its own right, to emanate light, as if it, and not its role in the overall dramatic situation, were most important to the author. Through taking on the power of illumination in this fashion, it makes us aware of the authorial personality who is creating the event, or rather recreating it, since obviously the memory must be a report from experience. Here the temporal perspective is vital to the way in which we read the incident; we must feel that it is something out of the past, illuminated by being recaptured. The autobiographical dimension is created by the clear indication of the fact that authorial memory is at work.

To illustrate the kind of description that I am talking about, I should like now to take a passage from Proust, another from Wolfe, and the third from a novel in which the so-called autobiographical dimension seems to be missing. Each of these passages describes approximately the same subject matter, and it is interesting to see the different ways it can be approached. Because the passage from Wolfe—it is taken from *Of Time and the River*—is in certain respects less complex than that from Proust, I begin with it.

The train toils slowly round the mountain grades, the short and powerful blasts of its squat funnel sound harsh and metallic against the sides of rocky cuts. One looks out the window and sees cut, bank, and gorge slide slowly past, the old rock wet and gleaming with the water of some buried mountain spring. The train goes slowly over the perilous and dizzy height of a wooden trestle; far below, the traveller can see and hear the clean foaming clamors of rock-bright mountain water; beside the track, before his little hut, a switchman stands looking at the train with the slow wondering gaze of the mountaineer. The little shack in which he lives is stuck to the very edge of the track above the steep and perilous ravine. His wife, a slattern with a hank of tight drawn hair, a snuff-stick in her mouth, and the same gaunt, slow wondering stare her husband has, stands in the doorway of the shack, holding a dirty little baby in her arms.

It is all so strange, so near, so far, terrible, beautiful, and instantly familiar, that it seems to the traveller that he must have known these people forever, that he must now stretch forth his hand to them from the windows and the rich and sumptuous luxury of the pullman car, that he must speak to them. And it seems to him that all the strange and bitter miracle of life—how, why, or in what way, he does not know—is in that instant greeting and farewell; for once seen, and lost the minute that he sees it, it is his forever and he can never forget it. And then the slow toiling train has passed these lives and faces and is gone, and there is something in his heart he cannot say.[11]

This passage occurs early in *Of Time and the River,* and is part of Eugene Gant's trip from Altamont to Harvard, where he goes to study playwriting. Like the two passages which follow, there is a kind of suspended animation between origin and destination, and what is occurring happens outside of the protagonist's life, and he reflects upon it. The passage *seems* to be

11. Thomas Wolfe, *Of Time and the River* (New York, 1935), p. 26.

set in the present tense. Actually, however, the use of the present helps perform a paradoxical function; it extends the action beyond present time, and bestows upon it a kind of archetypal quality, in making Eugene Gant's trip to Harvard representative of other trips, all such travels. Wolfe does not say that Eugene looks out of the window; he says that "*one* looks out the window"—that is, what Eugene is doing at this time, many others have done in other times.

The man, woman and infant at the wooden shack beside the right-of-way, glimpsed as they are for only a moment, remain frozen in time, motionless. It is a piece of time captured and preserved, as in a photograph. There is the scene: a mountain cut, a trestle, a switchman's shack, a man, woman, and child, and the traveler within the train watching, thinking of the meaning of this moment. Then, in the final sentence, the spell is broken, the train moves on, the scene passes out of sight, gone forever in time, yet permanently a part of the viewer's— and the author's—imagination. The author's ultimate objective has not been the scene beyond the windows, but the sensations of the man observing it and remembering it. By showing the man observing the scene, he is reliving the moment himself. The incident does little to further the narrative progression of Eugene Gant's trip from Altamont to Harvard; its primary importance is not even to show the kind of person Eugene was when he made the journey. His memory of *the moment itself* is what the author is chiefly concerned with, and in such a way as to make us very aware that he sees it—the viewer, what he is viewing, how he reacts to what he sees—archetypally.

Next, a passage from Proust, occurring in *Within a Budding Grove* as the young Marcel is traveling by train to the seacoast resort of Balbac:

The scenery became broken, abrupt, the train stopped at a little station between two mountains. Far down the gorge, on the edge of a hurrying stream, one could see only a solitary watch-house, deep-planted in the water which ran past on a level with its windows. If a person can be the product of a soil the peculiar charm of which one distinguishes in that person, more even than the peasant girl whom I had so desperately longed to see appear when I wandered by myself among the Méséglise way, in the woods of Roussainville, such a person must be the big girl whom I now saw emerge from the house and, climbing a path lighted by the first slanting rays of the sun, come towards the station carrying a jar of milk. In her valley from which its congregated summits hid the rest of the world, she could never see anyone save in these trains which stopped for a moment only. She passed down the line of windows, offering coffee and milk to a few awakened passengers. Purpled with the glow of morning, her face was rosier than the sky. I felt in her presence that desire to live which is reborn in us whenever we become conscious anew of beauty and of happiness. We invariably forget that these are individual qualities, and, substituting for them in our mind a conventional type at which we arrive by striking a sort of mean amongst the different faces that have taken our fancy, the pleasure we have known, we are left with mere abstract images which are lifeless and dull because they are lacking in precisely that element of novelty, different from anything we have known, that element which is proper to beauty and happiness. And we deliver on life a pessimistic judgment which we suppose to be fair, for we believed that we were taking into account when we formed it happiness and beauty, whereas in fact we left them out and replaced them by syntheses in which there is not a single atom of either. . . . Life would have seemed an exquisite thing to me if only I had been free to spend it, hour after hour, with her, to go with her to the stream, to the cow, to the train, to be always at her side, to feel that I was known to her, had my place in her thoughts. She would have initiated me into the delights of country life and of the first hours of the day. I signalled to her to give me some of her coffee. I felt that I must be noticed by her. She did not see me; I called to her. Above her body, which was of massive build, the complexion of her face was so burnished and so ruddy that she appeared almost as though I were looking at her through a lighted window. She had turned and was coming towards me; I could not take my eyes from her face which grew larger as she approached, like a sun which it was somehow possible to arrest in its course and drew towards one, letting itself be seen at close quarters, blinding the eyes with its blaze of red and gold. She fastened upon me her penetrating stare, but while the porters ran along the platform shutting doors the train had begun to move. I saw her leave the station and go down the hill to her home; it was broad daylight now; I was speeding away from the dawn. (I, 497–99)

The scene is very similar to Wolfe's. Though the young Marcel is "closer" to the milk-girl than Eugene Gant was to the mountain family—the train has stopped, Marcel can call to her, attempt to attract her attention—the point of both incidents is the same, having to do with the solitude of human beings in time. Characteristically, where Wolfe says that "there is something in his heart he cannot say." Proust plunges ahead, through the device of his first-person narrator, to say a great deal. He points out that the individual is normally trapped within the limitations of his own fixed customs, attitudes, and habits, with the barriers these impose upon the capacity for fresh experience. Because it breaks the routine of custom, the train trip also breaks the usual restriction of one's capacity for new experience, and one sees other human beings not as adjuncts to one's own subjective personality, but as individuals, so that they represent the possibility of new experience, new life. But the train moves on, the possibility is left behind, one remains oneself; with, however, the moment of time fixed and preserved in memory, independent of chronology: "For ever wilt thou love, and she be fair!"

The presence of the narrator, the adult Marcel, dominates the scene, of course, so that we are at least equally interested in what the first-person narrator thinks as in what has happened to young Marcel. However, the effect of the narrator's commentary is to universalize the experience, to compare it with other experiences possessing the same meaning. The near-encounter of Marcel with the milk-girl is made the occasion for a general observation, and Proust, like Wolfe, is ultimately more concerned with the meaning of the moment for its own sake than with its dramatic role in the journey on which young Marcel is embarked. We have momentarily forgotten all about going to Balbec.

At a moment such as this one in Proust's great novel, it is difficult to make a distinction between the authorial personality describing the event and the mind of the first-person narrator who serves here to tell us the authorial personality's thoughts about the long-ago encounter with the milk-girl. The narrator performs the role that in the Wolfe passage is filled by the author's commentary. In any event the result, so far as our sense of their being autobiographical passages goes, is the same: the immediate action is relegated to secondary importance, the meaning of the incident for the young Marcel is likewise under-played; and we are given the moment itself, its dimensions fully explored, standing out luminously, and directing our attention to the person for whom it thus stands out, the remembering authorial personality. We see Proust recapturing a past event, giving the occurrence order and meaning in the retelling by describing it as it happened and making his narrator speculate on its meaning.

The third passage that I want to cite is from *The Sun Also Rises*, by Ernest Hemingway:

We passed through a town and stopped in front of the posada, and the driver took on several packages. Then we started on again, and outside the town the road commenced to mount. We were going through farming country with rocky hills that sloped down into the fields. The grain-fields went up the hillsides. Now as we went higher there was a wind blowing the grain. The road was white and dusty, and the dust rose under the wheels and hung in the air behind us. The road climbed up into the hills and left the rich grain-fields below. Now there were only patches of grain on the bare hillsides and on each side of the water-courses. We turned sharply out to the side of the road to give room to pass a long string of six mules, following one after the other, hauling a high-hooded wagon loaded with freight. The wagon and the mules were covered with dust. Close behind was another string of mules and another wagon. This was loaded with lumber, and the arriero driving the mules leaned back and put on the thick wooden brakes as we passed. Up here the country was quite barren and the hills were rocky and hard-baked clay furrowed by the rain.

We came around a curve into a town, and on both sides opened out a sudden green valley. A stream went through the centre of the town and fields of grapes touched the houses.[12]

The ingredients of the passage are similar to those of the Proust and Wolfe passages. The narrator is describing a mountain scene. There is the same sense, though much less overtly noted, of the traveler's momentary awareness of the existence of people and places that lie beyond the customary limitations of his own habitual subjectivity. Where are the mule trains going? Who are those people? The arriero puts on the brake: the two discrete worlds notice each other's existence. Yet the passage does not, upon closer inspection, work in the same way at all. The scene is pointed ahead, in motion towards Burguete where Jake Barnes and Bill Gorton will go trout fishing. Time does not stop. The string of mules, followed by another, are passed en route, as the bus speeds by.

Hemingway devotes at least as much effort as Wolfe and Proust did to describing the scenery; the actual physical description, I think, is more memorable than either Proust's moun-

12. Ernest Hemingway, *The Sun Also Rises*, Scribner Library ed. (New York, 1954), pp. 105–06.

tain station stop or Wolfe's ravine with switchman's shack. Indeed it is almost unforgettable; were one to go traveling along that way, one would be instantly reminded of it. Yet oddly enough, though we may realize upon reflection that Hemingway is undoubtedly describing something from his own experience, we do not think of this at the time. The function of the passage is twofold: to show the two men traveling from Pamplona to Burguete, and to portray the calming effect of the mountain landscape upon Jake Barnes's nervous, tension-ridden sensibility. It achieves both ends.

This, however, is an end to it; the chief purpose served by the scene is to advance the novel, and we read the passage for its dramatic role. It possesses none of the quality of luminous revelation of the impact of a moment in time, nor of the redemption of that moment through an authorial personality's memory. Hemingway does not say, "now as *one* goes higher," as Wolfe would do, thus addressing the reader directly. He does not inject Jake Barnes as narrator to discuss the motivation and reasons for his feelings at the moment, and what they mean about these moments, as Proust would have done. Jake's role is that of the dramatic character for whom the action has meaning.

Hemingway makes no effort to set up a temporal perspective; Barnes is relating the story, but he is not telling it from a contrived and definite distance in time. Jake began his story as if it had happened a while ago, but by this time the effect is almost that of simultaneous narration, with the meaning resting entirely in what is happening at the moment. I do not mean by all this that the novel possesses no symbolic dimension, no universal quality; far from it. But it does so as a complete action, dramatically, and not at each interval along the way. The trip to Burguete, for example, does indeed have an archetypal design; seen in relation to the fiesta at Pamplona, it represents a journey back to Eden, a poignant interlude of escape from society and civilization, which cannot last. Yet whatever our experience of Hemingway's novel may be, *The Sun Also Rises* does not, I think, involve any active consciousness of an autobiographical element within it.

Now of course once we are familiar with Hemingway's life, we tend to regard all his fiction as extensions of his personality. We may catch ourselves thinking about Jake Barnes—and Frederic Henry, and Harry Morgan, and Robert Jordan, and Colonel Cantwell, and even Santiago—as if each were Hemingway. But this is not the same thing as autobiographical fiction. We have to ask, where does our knowledge come from? It comes, I believe, not from anything in the way the Hemingway novels are told, but from our familiarity with Hemingway's biography. We know that he liked bullfights, for instance; he wrote two works of nonfiction about them. When, therefore, Jake Barnes in *The Sun Also Rises* behaves, somewhat self-consciously, like a true *aficionado*, we say, Ah, there is Ernest writing about Ernest! But if we didn't already know this, there would be nothing in the way in which Hemingway described the bullfighting at Pamplona to suggest any relationship with the author's life. No remembering personality is at work making us sense such a relationship. Hemingway is not that kind of a writer, and when, in *Across the River and Into the Trees*, we catch Colonel Cantwell striking poses that we associate with the author's public personality, the fictional quality at once suffers. It is not autobiographical fiction, but fictionalized autobiography, which is to say that the artistic "suspension of disbelief" that is at the heart of our engagement in the literary image is lost, and we begin measuring what is going on by its literal faithfulness to "real life."

"Autobiography," writes Northrop Frye, "is another form

which merges with the novel by a series of insensible gradations. Most autobiographies are inspired by a creative, and therefore fictional, impulse to select only those events and experiences in the writer's life that go to build up an integrated pattern." [13] Supposedly, then, one might well be reading what one thought was autobiography, when in reality it was fiction; or, what is more to the point, what one thought was fiction but was really autobiography. Could we draw a kind of spectrum, perhaps, with, let us say, a quite factual work such as General U. S. Grant's *Memoirs* at one pole, and next to that a book such as Edward John Trelawny's *Adventures of a Younger Son,* which though it purports to be autobiographical is widely imaginary, followed by Proust's novel and at the opposite pole from the factual memoir, a novel such as *The Ambassadors?* No one, I think, has ever seriously accused General Grant of consciously making up his facts as he went along, and no critical account of James's novel that I have seen has stressed autobiographical overtones.

Such a spectrum, it seems to me, would be close to nonsensical. The fact that Grant dealt with material which other accounts show is historically accurate, while Trelawny for the most part invented his supposedly true-to-life material, does not importantly differentiate the works so far as the way that we are made to read them is concerned. They are autobiographical memoirs not because the material in them is "true," but because of the way they are written. The logic they follow is that of "life," and they are basically unselective in their details. The autobiographer may or may not, as Mr. Frye says, choose only those details that fit into an integrated pattern, but the pattern itself owes its fidelity to historical chance, to actual events. There

13. Northrop Frye, *Anatomy of Criticism* (Princeton, N.J., 1957), p. 307.

is little or no attempt at real characterization, in the fictional sense. Even Trelawny, who depicts himself in a light very different from that which objective observation would verify, was not writing fictional characterization. The credibility of his work is dependent at all times on the fact, obvious to us from the way that he tells an event, that it "happened," and when as often is the case we sense that something did not really happen at all, we label it as a lie and read it for its psychological revelation of the author.

In *Remembrance of Things Past,* by contrast, the logic is imaginative, the use of details is selective, and the emphasis is all on characterization, on the "probable impossible." The autobiographical dimension comes in not because any of the events actually "happened," but because the overall imaginative ordering involves the experience of memory, of recapture—the authorial personality looking at his material from the perspective of time, and understanding it through remembering it.

One might object, "But couldn't this be true of literal autobiography as well?" Certainly; but in that case it would not be autobiography but autobiographical fiction—which is evidently precisely what *Remembrance of Things Past* is.

The *Memoirs* of U. S. Grant involve the selection and arrangement of the facts derived from the author's memory, but the narrative depends for suspense and interest not on any inherent development of characterization and situation, but an always verifiable and documented relationship to attitudes, feelings, and interests of the reader that lie outside the narrative itself and in historical, political, and social fact. If the reader did not already know who General Grant was, or what the Civil War was, the author's account would be of relatively little interest. The autobiographical novelist, by contrast, like any other kind of novelist, creates his meaning, his documentation, as he goes along, and the reader's participation is of a different and more imaginative order entirely.

A novel such as *Remembrance of Things Past* depends for suspense and meaning on the reader's knowing that it was written by the central character. When we see Marcel in Combray and Paris making his first awkward and unsuccessful attempts at literary creation, and when we see him conducting his involved and ultimately fruitless and frustrated inquiries into society and love, we know that in the end he will succeed in giving purpose and meaning to his life, and we read on in order to find out how he manages this. Of course the book we are reading proves that he managed it, and is also an abundant demonstration of how he did so. But that is not enough; at the close we must feel that Marcel has begun to emerge from his frustration and confusion. Otherwise the long, extensive narrative would seem pointless and without purpose. The novel therefore ends, as it were, at the point where it begins, which involves the old paradox that the novel itself is part of the fiction!

For the meaning of Proust's novel this is no more than appropriate, because what Marcel learns is that nothing else in time is real except its redemption in art. The novel is thus a kind of closed system, and whatever exists must be made to fit into it.

For all its brilliance, however, this aspect of Proust's great masterwork is not entirely convincing. Most readers are likely to be reluctant to go along with this judgment, for though there may be considerable disagreement as to the nature of reality, and of its meaning for the individual human being, most of us are not so willing as Proust to declare that only in art can human time be redeemed.

In this respect it is interesting to compare Proust with his illustrious compatriot of a hundred years previous, Stendhal. If Proust's great novel constitutes a search for lost time, and if Marcel discovers, at the end, that time can be redeemed and the past recaptured in art, he is discovering, in a sense, no more than what Stendhal knew in 1840 when he wrote these words to Balzac:

> Death causes us to exchange rôles with such people [as Metternich]. They can do anything to our bodies during their lives, but at the moment of death oblivion enfolds them forever. Who will speak of M. de Villèle, or of M. de Martignac, in a hundred years? M. de Talleyrand himself will be saved only by his *Memoires*, if he has left any good ones; whereas *Le Roman Comique* is today what *Le Père Goriot* will be in 1980. It is Scarron who keeps us familiar with the name of that Rothschild of his day, M. de Montauron, who was also, at a cost of fifty louis, the patron of Corneille.[14]

". . . that frightful quantity of *I*'s and *me*'s!" Stendhal wrote, contemplating the task of recreating his whole life in a book; but he knew what Proust knew also when he wrote that "anything we have not had to decipher and clarify by our own personal effort, anything that was clear before we intervened, is not our own. Nothing comes from ourselves but that which we draw out of the obscurity within us and which is unknown to others." (II, 1002) What Stendhal called Egotism was for Proust the Book of Himself, and neither writer was really guilty of the indulgent worship of self. Rather, both these French writers, taking their key perhaps from the Cartesian principle that predicates the universe upon the premise that the self exists, embarked on what is essentially an artistic process of recreating themselves as works of art.

14. Stendhal, Letter, "To Honoré de Balzac," in *To the Happy Few: Selected Letters of Stendhal*, trans. Norman Cameron (New York, 1952), p. 373.

I mean this in the most literal sense. Those several Marcels of *Remembrance of Things Past*—the youth growing up in Combray, the narrator telling about him, the authorial personality whose presence we sense—are none of them the literal, biographical Proust, though they contain so much of him; they are achieved artistic characterization. And as for Stendhal, as Robert Adams declares:

"Beylism" is the art of creating a man named Beyle, who shall in turn be capable of creating men named Julien Sorel and Fabrizio del Dongo. And the self thus created is not dead, formal, and static; it includes resources of experience, dramatic stratagems, and caves of memory. It includes, that is, processes for searching out fresh reality-forms, for structuring them, and for recovering and transforming them.[15]

Proust evolved, for his purposes, a gigantic architectonic structure in which the identity, even while moving steadily forward in time toward the moment of realization for which all that preceded it was "a vocation," doubles back upon itself and its time and place to give form and meaning to whatever it has encompassed. For Stendhal no such formal structuring took place; his work is scattered, even chaotic, and takes unity and meaning primarily from the impress of his personality.

All the same let us admit that there was a price to be paid by Proust for the unity of form and meaning with which he was able to invest his world. "Truth," its narrator declares in a sentence already quoted once before in this chapter, "will begin only when the writer takes two different objects, establishes their relationship—analogous in the world of art to the sole relationship in the world of science, the law of cause and effect—and encloses them in the necessary rings of a beautiful style, or even when, like life itself, comparing similar qualities

15. Robert M. Adams, *Stendhal: Notes on a Novelist* (New York, 1959), p. 218.

in two sensations, he makes their essential nature stand out clearly by joining them in a metaphor, in order to remove them from the contingencies of time, and links them together with the indescribable bond of an alliance of words." (II, 1008–09) A beautiful description of the writer's art, and yet—does this not point to the principal defect in Proust's great novel, which is to say, a tendency toward overorganization, an occasional forcing of experience into a unity that is not really convincing? The Proustian style, beautiful, flowing, all-encompassing, with long sentences that weave complex experience into form and pattern, seems sometimes to join and to assimilate what cannot after all really be assimilated, so that not the relationship between two sensations, but the effort of the metaphor is what strikes us. In short, to force Marcel's experience into general meaning, Proust sometimes strains relationships, asserts similarity when none is present, ascribes meaning at the expense of plausibility.

Do we, after all, finally believe the Proustian ordering of experience? Do we accept the Proustian definition of love? Or do we not instead feel that, for all the stunning revelation it affords along the way, it is ultimately incomplete, even false? And do we not have the feeling that sometimes Proust is forcing his world into his thesis, as when for example he makes Saint Loup turn into a homosexual? Do we really believe that the Prince de Guermantes would ever have married Madame Verdurin? That, for all that it is painstakingly and cunningly prepared, the signature of Gilberte could ever have been misread by a telegraph clerk as being that of Albertine? That Marcel could possibly have kept Albertine a prisoner-mistress in his apartment as he says he did?

At times like these we draw back, withhold our credulity; and we suddenly find ourselves thinking then, not of Marcel, not of the implied narrator of the novel, not of the authorial personality whom Proust has created, but instead of the biographical real-life Marcel Proust, the homosexual who kept his vice secret from the personality image of himself he was creating but who has suddenly and unwittingly revealed himself to us. For that moment the artistry fails, and we see Proust forcing the masculine Saint Loup to share his vice, transposing Guido Agostinelli into a woman. And while we soon re-enter the magnificent fictional world of the *Remembrance of Things Past*, we do not forget this. So that when the story is complete, and Marcel is ready to begin writing the novel we have just finished reading, we ask ourselves whether it was not perhaps precisely this homosexuality that made Proust see sexual love as cruel, vain, and ultimately meaningless. For all its stunning beauty, the formal unity of Proust's great novel has to a certain extent been achieved at the expense of credibility; the real-life documentation has been falsified in part.

Whatever else may be said of Stendhal, of this fault he is almost never guilty. Often we may feel that Stendhal is manipulating his characters to display his wit; at these moments we are quite conscious of the Stendhalism personality telling the story. But there is almost never any feeling of falsification, of an effect created at the expense of plausibility. Stendhal, the personage created by Beyle, is always honest and open with us. That he has his little vanities, that he is not above changing small facts in order to make an impression on us, is not disconcerting; this is all part of the game. But he never lies about reality. He never tries to make life simpler, or more tidy, than it is. Stendhal conceals nothing. The documentation of the world is never forced into a form into which it will not fit of its own accord, in order to create an esthetic unity at the expense of being faithful to experience. When Stendhal declares that his goal is "the *truths* of the human heart," he means exactly that.

Of course we cannot equate Stendhal's assortment of novels completed and uncompleted, journals, memoirs, histories, biographies, travel books, and so forth with the unified and mastered artistic experience that is *Remembrance of Things Past*. As already noted, Stendhal did not retire to a cork-lined room; his exile at Civitavecchia was not the occasion for his writing of his greatest fiction. He did that in Paris, writing at breakneck speed even while continuing to go out in society. Stendhal found his times absurd, but also delightful, and did not care to give up life for art. Marcel Proust was willing to do this, and so we have not only *Swann's Way* but the other six books as well.

We are told that when *Swann's Way* first appeared, one of the book's admirers was Henry James. That James, who supposedly cared so little for the first person singular in the writing of fiction, should have enjoyed the Proustian method might seem strange, if it were not that unlike some of his disciples, Henry James, as we well know, never let abstract theories get in the way of the appreciation of literature. What he must have enjoyed, we can guess, was above all the style: the weaving of complex experience into a unified artistic whole through the long, linking resources of metaphor. And perhaps he recognized in Proust what we recognize in both of them and their work (and in the writings of Stendhal as well): that here are novelists whose great personalities are stamped on everything they wrote, because for all three of them the mere relating of events was not enough, since all three knew so well what James meant when he wrote that "one's work should have composition, because composition alone is positive beauty." [16]

16. Henry James, "Preface to *The Ambassadors*," in R. P. Blackmur ed., *The Art of the Novel*, Scribner Library ed. (New York, 1934), p. 319.

SIX · A Portrait
of a Highly Visible Artist

A CCOUNTS differ, the biographers of both Marcel Proust
and James Joyce tell us, as to what transpired at that famous party in Paris in 1920 when the still young twentieth
century's two greatest novelists met for the one and only time
in their lives. One report is that they discussed their illnesses—
Joyce's eyes hurt, Proust had a bad stomach ache; another is
that they discussed truffles; still another version has it that each
man announced that he had never read anything by the other.
It is agreed that they took a cab together, that Proust got out
at his apartment and Joyce continued on home. "Proust's day
was just beginning. Mine was at an end," Joyce said.[1]

That these two writers had little to say to each other is
scarcely surprising. Their books are likewise polarities. It is not
too farfetched to say that *Remembrance of Things Past* represents the culmination of one kind of fictional mode, while
Ulysses represents the equally ultimate statement of another and
antithetical mode. Proust stretches and extends sentence order
and syntax to the utmost extent, enlarging the pattern of language to embrace and absorb an exhaustively complex experience, in order to achieve what is finally a wholly subjective

1. See Richard Ellmann, *James Joyce* (New York, 1959), pp. 523–24, and
George D. Painter, *Proust: The Later Years* (Boston, 1965), pp. 340–42, for
accounts of this meeting by the major biographers of each man.

crisis of meaning—the conviction that all time and experience exist within the single recreated imagination of one man. Joyce, by contrast, breaks up and fragments the pattern of language in order to divide human awareness into immediate and unmediated bursts of consciousness, in order to describe a day, a city, two very different men and a woman—the objective and concrete look of external experience. And when the day is done, his artist has learned to look not inside himself for reality, but outside at the world.

In the previous chapter I have sought to show how the unity that the protagonist of Proust's great novel recognizes in all his experience, and recreates in the work of art that describes his quest for that meaning, resides in the articulated and dramatized presence of the authorial personality telling his narrator's story, and how the relationship between that authorial personality and the material he remembers and recreates gives the book much of its excitement for us. I want now to try to show that in the novels of James Joyce, the same is largely true: to show the extent to which Joyce's two major works of fiction depend for their meaning on his role as teller in the tale. What I shall have to say is not particularly new in its details; but I do hope that the emphases I give to already well-covered material will be of some use in helping to understand better what is ultimately impossible ever to understand fully: of what our experience of reading these novels consists.

Stately, plump Buck Mulligan and his English friend Haines are having lunch, and the talk turns to Stephen Dedalus. Mulligan munches on a buttered biscuit:

—Ten years, he said, chewing and laughing. He is going to write something in ten years.

—Seems a long way off, Haines said, thoughtfully lifting his spoon. Still, I shouldn't wonder if he did after all. (p. 249)[2]

The conversation leads back to trivia, and we do not again meet either these two gentlemen, or Stephen himself, until much later in *Ulysses*. But before the passage closes we are informed that in the harbor of Dublin that day is the "three-masted schooner *Rosevean* from Bridgwater with bricks."

Earlier we have seen that schooner, moving silently, "homing, upstream, silently moving, a silent ship," as Stephen Dedalus finishes a long walk along the shore before proceeding townward. (p. 51) And much later that evening, when an exhausted and brain-numbed Stephen is brought by Leopold Bloom into a cabman's shelter for coffee and food, a half-drunken, timeworn old sailor from that same *Rosevean* lurches clumsily about the little restaurant and tells partly incoherent and entirely uninteresting tales about his years of sailing the seven seas.

In James Joyce's first novel, *A Portrait of the Artist as a Young Man*, another sailing ship figures prominently in the diary that young Stephen Dedalus keeps as he prepares to leave the land of his fathers for the life of the artist in exile that he wishes to be. In this book the ship is described in somewhat less prosaic tones than in *Ulysses*:

April 16. Away! Away!
    The spell of arms and voices: the white arms of roads, their promise of close embraces and the black arms of tall ships that stand against the moon, their tales of distant nations. They are held out to say: We are alone—come. And the voices say with them: We are your kinsmen. And the air is thick with their company as they call to me, their

2. James Joyce, *Ulysses*, Modern Library ed. (New York, 1961). All quotations from the book are taken from this edition, and are given parenthetically.

kinsman, making ready to go, shaking the wings of their exultant and terrible youth. (p. 253)[3]

If one is a Joycean and a critic, there are numerous ways that one might go about the business of sizing up the import of the good ship *Rosevean*. The ship, one could say, is setting forth as *A Portrait* closes, speeding the young artist on his way. One might even note that on the very first page of *A Portrait* young Dedalus dances the sailor's hornpipe as his mother plays the piano; a prophecy of things to come, it would appear. But in *Ulysses* Stephen Dedalus is back in Dublin, as yet far from "forging in the smithy of my soul the uncreated conscience of my race" (p. 253) as he had planned to do in *A Portrait,* and the ship coming back to port signifies the return of his artistic muse to the city where it will find spiritual, if not physical, habitation. Furthermore, the ship in *Ulysses* is a much more worldy ship, and carries bricks back home, not proud young artists going forth, and in *Ulysses* Stephen Dedalus learns that artificers, however fabulous, build labyrinths with bricks, some imported, not with abstract theories of design; that life without Plumtree's Potted Meat is incomplete, no matter how delightful the divine ambrosia; and so the transformation of a sailing ship from a romantic silhouette against the moon into a homeward-bound merchant vessel symbolizes the transformation of Stephen from the esthete of *A Portrait* to the flesh-and-blood artist he is destined to be.

Not only that, but the ship is named the *Rosevean;* we all know about the symbolic rose, the wild one that blooms on the little green place on page 7 of *A Portrait;* and the sacred rose

3. James Joyce, *A Portrait of the Artist as a Young Man*, Compass Books ed. (New York, 1961). All quotations from the book are taken from this edition, and are given parenthetically.

of the rosary that Dante Alighieri cultivated so well; and the Dantesque girl dressed in rose; and the *Rose of Castille* that is the joke Lenahan tells at the newspaper office; and Gerty Mc-Dowell, "delicate as the faintest rosebloom"; and the rose gardens that Molly (the flowers that Bloom in the spring) dreamed of as she reaffirmed her Yes to life at the close of *Ulysses;* and so on. With Hanley's concordance to Ulysses one could take this on indefinitely. But I lack the talent; I yield to William York Tindall, who does not.

James Joyce has been the greatest single boon to literary symbol-hunting since Caroline Spurgeon discovered Shakespeare; indeed, one must go all the way back to Dante and Chaucer to find a writer who is as kind to symbol-seekers as Joyce. Nor is Joyce's attractiveness for this kind of scholarship merely accidental; not only did he intend it thus, but he collaborated with various publicity agents, notably Stuart Gilbert, in setting forth the basic rules and nomenclature so that the hunt could begin at once. Symbolatry, that besetting sin of medievalists and post-Parnassian French poets, becomes with the advent of James Joyce the literary equivalent of what radio-telescopes have meant to astronomers and molded plastic to toy manufacturers.

There is of course nothing innately unhealthy about a symbol or any other kind of artistic pun; it is a species of good clean sport, and if Joyce's final work, *Finnegans Wake,* survives its century that will in large part be because of the amusement the book affords English professors. Not only, as Joyce pointed out, was the Holy Roman Church founded upon a pun, but equally are most of the major intellectual movements of our own times. Freudianism would be no science at all without the pun; Jungian archetypal pattern is based on the fact that one activity unconsciously resembles another; even the mystique of

Marxism greatly depends on the imaginative associations, in English at least, of the words "community," "common," and "communion."

One can, in short, no more divorce the reading of the novels of James Joyce from an awareness of and interest in symbolism and puns than one can separate the medieval Roman Catholic church and the *Divine Comedy*. But what, after all, do symbols and puns mean about *Ulysses*? What is their function? They show correspondences, unite apparently disparate events and thoughts, characterize people and activities; provide emphasis and intensification; help to accumulate experience; add richness, depth, humor, irony; confer meaning. All these are important; to the reader of Joyce they are essential.

Yet the involved symbolism and elaborate wordplay in Joyce's fiction have another function, one not so often noted, but of great importance to the artistry of *A Portrait* and *Ulysses* both. They are devices—not the only ones, but extremely important ones—for making and keeping us aware, at all points in both novels, of the presence of the author. For neither of these two novels is the creation of an effaced, invisible artist; they are told to us by an author who has a talent for puns. And unless we realize they are (which indeed we cannot for a moment help but do), they would mean little or nothing to us. In *Ulysses*, for example, not three but four main personalities are at work: Stephen Dedalus, Leopold Bloom, Molly Bloom, and the author whose name appears on the title page and whom we recognize as such an artist as Stephen Dedalus will eventually become.

The author of the *Portrait* and *Ulysses* is an "effaced narrator" only in that he never uses the pronoun "I" to tell his story; in point of fact he is very much *not* effaced, very much present and active, and highly interested in letting the reader know he is there. The symbols he keeps using and the puns he keeps making are one way he does this. There are others, including the dropping of hints, as in the dialogue between Mulligan and Haines, quoted earlier, which immediately precedes the comment on the schooner *Rosevean* in Ulysses. Buck Mulligan's jest about Stephen's plans to write something in ten years, of course, is typical of Mulligan, and helps to show the jealousy Mulligan entertains for Stephen. But Haines's reply, made "thoughtfully," that "I shouldn't wonder if he did after all," is not a device of characterization, and can in no way advance the literal plot situation; its function is to impress upon us the fact that Stephen Dedalus will not always be the *artist manqué* that he is in *Ulysses,* and the proof is the book one is now reading. Stephen will not write *Ulysses* in ten years; but the author knows that most of his readers will be quite aware that the final page of *A Portrait* bears the notation "Dublin, 1904. Trieste, 1914."

So much deserved praise has been expended on James Joyce by his admirers—and of all twentieth-century literary cultists, the Joyceans are the most numerous and the most intense, outdoing even the Jamesians in this respect—for his marvelous scenic ability, his skill at creating the full sensory dimensions of a scene ("Local colour. Work in all you know.") that the fact that the Joyce novels are narrated generally goes unremarked. Whatever Stephen Dedalus' shortcomings in dealing with the common clay of everyday experience, they are not James Joyce's. "In the creation of his background—the city of Dublin on June 16, 1904—Joyce has achieved an amazing air of reality, a reality which proceeds not from ordinary external description but from a reliance upon the psychological sensations presented to the mind," Richard M. Kain declares. "Dublin is nowhere described; but, as the reader follows the characters through the streets, into lunch-joint, library, newspaper office, hospital, bar, and brothel, he feels that he knows Dublin as a resident would know it." [4] Joyce's technique, or more properly his variety of techniques, is unexcelled in the ability to represent the concrete, palpable shape and form of recreated life.

Yet in and through this very virtuosity, of course, not only is the reader of both *A Portrait* and *Ulysses* fully conscious, as he reads, that he is immersed not in "life" but in "art," and a very specific and self-conscious art at that, but he is perhaps more nearly conscious of this than in the work of any other writer of fiction in the twentieth century. Not only is there no "illusion of reality," in the sense that the reader is supposed to forget altogether that he is reading fiction and become involved in the story as if it were real life itself, but the whole is intentionally and inescapably a tremendous virtuoso performance by one of the greatest impresarios of language ever to write fiction. Consider for example an episode such as the retreat in *A Portrait,* in which Stephen listens to Father Arnall's hell-fire sermons. We become caught up in the sermon; we imagine the effect it must be having on the guilt-ridden young Stephen; but at the same time we art captivated by the literary artistry of the whole thing:

Ever to be in hell, never to be in heaven; ever to be shut off from the presence of God, never to enjoy the beatific vision; ever to be eaten with flames, gnawed with vermin, goaded with burning spikes, never to be freed from those pains; ever to have the conscience upbraid one, the memory enrage, the mind filled with darkness and despair, never to escape; ever to curse and revile the foul demons who gloat fiendishly over the misery of their dupes, never to behold the shining raiment of the blessed spirits; ever to cry out of the abyss of fire to God for an instant, a single instant, of respite from such awful agony, never to receive, even for an instant, God's pardon; ever to suffer, never to enjoy; ever to be damned, never to be saved; ever never; ever, never. . . . (pp. 132–33)

---

4. Richard M. Kain, *Fabulous Voyager: A Study of James Joyce's "Ulysses"* (New York, 1959), p. 20.

How eloquently he brings it off, one thinks, noting the rhetorical cadence, the matched and the contrasted rhythms, the excellent imitation of ecclesiastical prose.[5] One could no more be unconscious of the virtuosity of the passage, and therefore of the presence of the virtuoso who created it, than one could read Father Mapple's equally eloquent sermon in *Moby-Dick* without marveling at Melville's skill even while sensing what the sermon must mean for Ishmael, who is listening.

Or consider an incident of a somewhat less spiritually exalted nature, that in *Ulysses* in which Leopold Bloom, having breakfasted on kidney, goes out to the jakes for his morning evacuation. Bloom settles down, begins reading the story by Mr. Philip Beaufoy, of Playgoers' Club, London, entitled "Matcham's Masterstroke," speculates on the rewards of an authorial career, recalls a dance and Molly's behavior there, and all the while performs his natural functions. It is surely one of the most comical scenes in all of modern fiction, and Bloom is magnificently characterized. At no point does the author intrude upon the apparent objectivity of the description. Yet so brilliant is the *tour de force* that one cannot read the episode without thinking of Joyce's skill in imagining and writing it, and one cannot help visualizing how much Joyce must have enjoyed creating it. Not only, then, does the scene advance Bloom's characterization; it also enhances our admiration for the author's highly earthy sense of humor—we marvel at his audacity in doing it at all. And our awareness that the author of *Ulysses* does possess the kind of imagination to create such a scene will be essential to the understanding of the meaning of *Ulysses*.

5. See Kevin Sullivan, *Joyce Among the Jesuits* (New York, 1958), pp. 134–42, for an excellent account of Joyce's use of ecclesiastical material for this portion of *A Portrait*.

The whole question of the author as virtuoso is, when considered in this way, more than somewhat obvious, and few would dispute the fact that in this sense the author is present and that the reader is aware of his presence. What is important for my purposes, however, is not simply the author's presence, but the formal, esthetic necessity of it. Once again, I am not talking about biography, but about the *form of fiction,* the relationship between the fiction as presented and the meaning it can embody for the reader.

With certain exceptions, in particular Mr. S. L. Goldberg's notable *The Classical Temper,* comparatively little attention has been paid to this relationship. Biographical studies have more or less assumed the autobiographical nature of Joyce's novels, especially *A Portrait,* and have indeed been zealous in demonstrating the differences between the actual events of Joyce's life and the experience described in *A Portrait of the Artist as a Young Man,* without pausing to consider what those changes might mean, or why they are there.

Much critical attention, particularly from the point of view of theory, has been devoted to the statement of Stephen Dedalus' esthetics in *A Portrait,* with its implied question of whether Stephen stands for James, and thus whether *A Portrait* is straightforward "autobiographical fiction," after the manner of Thomas Wolfe or Samuel Butler, or whether the artist being described is, as Joyce insisted, indeed a very young man, and depicted in very ironical tones. Similarly, there are biographical and even geographical studies of *Ulysses,* and there are critical studies which attempt, from various points of departure and with greatly differing premises, to analyze the work as a novel. Frequently, these studies *assume* a relationship between Stephen and Joyce, even assume that the reader is supposed to know that

Stephen, or someone like him, eventually wrote *Ulysses*, but they do not give much thought to how one can legitimately assume this, or what the assumption means about the way the novel is constructed. I want to consider just those matters: how do we know that either of Joyce's novels is, in part or in whole, autobiographical; what does such a relationship involve insofar as the way we read the two novels are concerned; and what in turn all this has to do with Stephen Dedalus' famous discussion of literary modes.

First, the often quoted passage itself:

Lessing, said Stephen, should not have taken a group of statues to write of. The art, being inferior, does not present the forms I spoke of distinguished clearly one from another. Even in literature, the highest and most spiritual art, the forms are often confused. The lyrical form is in fact the simplest verbal vesture of an instant of emotion, a rhythmical cry such as ages ago cheered on the man who pulled at the oar or dragged stones up a slope. He who utters it is more conscious of the instant of emotion than of himself as feeling emotion. The simplest epical form is seen emerging out of lyrical literature when the artist prolongs and broods upon himself as the centre of an epical event and this form progresses till the centre of emotional gravity is equidistant from the artist himself and from others. The narrative is no longer purely personal. The personality of the artist passes into the narration itself, flowing round and round the persons and the action like a vital sea. This progress you will see easily in that old English ballad *Turpin Hero* which begins in the first person and ends in the third person. The dramatic form is reached when the vitality which has flowed and eddied round each person fills every person with such vital force that he or she assumes a proper and intangible esthetic life. The personality of the artist, at first a cry or a cadence or a mood and then a fluid and lambent narrative, finally refines itself out of existence, impersonalises itself, so to speak. The esthetic image in the dramatic form is life purified in and reprojected from the human imagination. The mystery of esthetic like that of material creation is accomplished.

The artist, like the God of the creation, remains within or behind or beyond or above his handiwork, invisible, refined out of existence, indifferent, paring his fingernails. (pp. 214–15)

The image of the Godlike artist standing aloof and indifferent, paring his fingernails, while the work he has created bears no part of himself, has inspired many hundreds of pages of Joyce criticism. What has been less noticed, however, is a remark that Stephen makes a bit earlier in his conversation with Lynch: "The image, it is clear, must be set between the mind or sense of the artist himself and the mind or senses of others." (p. 213) In other words, there is in every novel a relationship in which the reader and the novelist engage, and which is the novel itself; and the terms in which this novel, this artistic image of human experience, is to be read, must be agreed upon in order for it to be read at all. The novel is a genre; it is not life, but an image of life, possessing, in Stephen's terms, wholeness, harmony and radiance. Like Dr. Johnson's eighteenth-century playgoer, the reader of the novel knows very well that he is not viewing real life, but a work of artistic imagining. He knows too that it is the product of a single artist's imagination, and in this sense, of course, there can be no "invisible artist"—certainly James Joyce had no desire to be such a person, even if it were possible.

Not only is the reader thoroughly aware of the "artificiality" of what he is reading, the fact that it is artifice and not life itself, but he is also and equally aware that he is being *told* the story. We know, in other words, that someone is *telling* us *A Portrait of the Artist as a Young Man*.

In view of all that has been written about "lyric, epic, and dramatic" and the "invisible artist" as these concern Joyce's novels, the importance of this storytelling relationship may not at first be realized. It is there, however, and it is vital to the meaning of the novel, and I want now, at the risk of being even more obvious and also tedious, to examine in some detail the way *A Portrait* begins.

There is, first of all, the title, which informs us that the novel is going to be about an artist, and also that he will be a youthful artist. When therefore we encounter, in the first paragraph, a child, our expectation is that the child will be the artist in question, and that we shall be reading the account of the child's progress toward the role of artist. "Once upon a time," it begins, the traditional formula for storytelling. "Once upon a time and a very good time it was there was a moocow coming down along the road and this moocow that was down along the road met a nicens little boy named baby tuckoo. . . ." (p. 7) The beginning of a story, told to the reader by a narrator, and which the reader at once accepts. With the second paragraph a complication is introduced: "His father told him that story: his father looked at him through a glass: he had a hairy face." So it is not a story told by a narrator that the reader will get; there is going to be a character, a focus of consciousness, who will remember and possess the experience that the story will contain, and who will transmit that experience to us. Not merely what happens, then, but what this focal character thinks and feels about what happens, will be involved.

As yet, we do not know anything more about this focal character, though the title of the novel has led us to expect that he will be an artist as a youth—whose experience, after all, is he remembering, and why? So far he is only baby tuckoo, as we learn in the next paragraph, and this baby tuckoo sings a song about how "the wild rose blossoms" and "the green wothe botheth." Why, however, is the song given in correct English as first:

> "O, the wild rose blossoms
> On the little green place"

and then, once our character informs us that "He sang that song. That was his song," why is it repeated in baby talk?

> O, the green wothe botheth.

Why indeed? Not only to make that symbolic point about green roses and artifice. The juxtaposition, the contrast, helps establish the fact at the outset that there is a difference in consciousness between the teller of the story, who uses mature English, and the focal character when he was undergoing the experience of singing the song, and could speak only very inexpertly. "He sang that song. That was his song." The words are those of an older person, not delivered in baby talk, yet the syntax, the method of thinking, are those of the child. To the extent that he will act, be acted upon, think, feel, know, we get him as he was at the time. The person telling the story will not be a developing character himself; we are not going to be told what he thinks and feels. Instead he is going to serve as our narrator, using his language and his insight to direct, form, and bring into proper focus what happens. Our expectations—they are almost automatic, and we think of them scarcely if at all, for from long practice we are accustomed to reading novels—are confirmed by the next paragraph: "When you wet the bed, first it is warm then it gets cold. His mother puts on the oilsheet. That had the queer smell." (7) Again, the syntax, the vocabulary, the mode of thinking of a child, though with no childish misspellings and mispronunciations. But a somewhat older child than the child of the first four paragraphs; baby tuckoo could not have thought "That had the queer smell." The reflection upon the experience of bedwetting, too, is considerably more subtle; it involves the capacity to remember. So the focal character, the "he," is growing a little older, and we shall not be reading about his babyhood for very long. Instead our story teller is moving along swiftly. We are given, in rapid succession, several more episodes from the life of the central character—his name is Stephen, we learn in one of them—and each is more complex than the previous. He dances the hornpipe while his uncle and aunt clap. His aunt has brushes named for Michael Davitt and Parnell. There is a girl named Eileen who lives nearby.

Then we get two more incidents of much greater emotional complexity than anything yet encountered. Stephen has done something wrong, and has hidden under the table; apparently something involving marrying Eileen, since the statement that he hid under the table follows directly upon that thought. He will apologize, his mother says, and his aunt Dante adds, "O, if not, the eagles will come and pull out his eyes." (p. 8) So we have not only awareness of consciousness, awareness of other people, but *guilt* concerning his relationship to them. This is immediately followed by a refrain, which Stephen makes into a song, twice repeated:

> Pull out his eyes,
> Apologize,
> Apologize,
> Pull out his eyes.
>
> Apologize,
> Pull out his eyes,
> Pull out his eyes,
> Apologize. (p. 8)

Stephen has made something into poetry, or at any event into rhyme; out of the emotion involved in his still-dawning life, he is creating art, in that, in momentary detachment and objectivity, he is manipulating words and lines to see how they sound in differing relationship to each other. He is by this stage of his development sufficiently aware of the difference between his own consciousness and his external experience to reflect upon it, make a refrain of it.

The storyteller is only showing us Stephen; he is not addressing us by saying "Once upon a time." Even so, we know he is there and the effect of his having revealed to us, in succession, a group of incidents in Stephen's consciousness, each of greater complexity than the previous, is not only to tell us that Stephen is growing up, but also to reinforce this sense we have held from the outset: that a relationship exists between the storyteller and the focal character, a relationship involving memory. The storyteller is re-creating. Those incidents are not random incidents; they are in chronological order, from earliest to latest, moving from simple hearing and identification toward more complex associations of guilt, possibly involving sex, the need for apology, and the first crude but prophetic conversion of experience into art. They have therefore been *selected*, obviously, to demonstrate just such a development in Stephen's mind. We begin to see what the storyteller is doing, for the orderly, chronological arrangement, instead of mere random gusts of memory, keeps us quite aware of the fact that he is telling us the story of Stephen, and that he will probably expand and greatly elaborate on the developing consciousness of Stephen in the pages ahead. (Though to what effect we do not yet know, unless the conjunction of the novel's title and the fact that Stephen has already made a rhyme out of his experience gives us any indication.) Thus, by this point in the novel, the second page, we are as readers already fully taking part in a complex formal relationship. A story of a young boy, showing his development of his consciousness, is being told to us by a storyteller who most probably was once that young boy.

If we have any doubts concerning the identity of that storyteller—by now we may call him the novelist—they are removed by the paragraph which begins immediately afterward:

The wide playgrounds were swarming with boys. All were shouting and the prefects urged them on with strong cries. The evening air was pale and chilly and after every charge and thud of the footballers the greasy leather orb flew like a heavy bird through the grey light. He kept on the fringe of his line, out of sight of his prefect, out of the reach of the rude feet, feigning to run now and then. He felt his body small and weak amid the throng of players and his eyes were weak and watery. Rody Kickham was not like that: he would be captain of the third line all the fellows said. (p. 8)

Here the language and the syntax start out clearly as that of an adult; Stephen would never have used an expression such as "the greasy leather orb" or say that it "flew like a heavy bird through the grey light." That is quite mature, narrated prose. But with the last sentence the language and syntax abruptly switch back to that of the small child. Why? Because the last sentence is what Stephen *thinks* to himself, while the preceding sentences are what Stephen *feels*. To show what Stephen says to himself, Stephen's own words are appropriate and necessary. But to show what Stephen is feeling, his simple vocabulary will not do at all. Stephen would surely never think to call a football anything but a football; but the word itself cannot convey how Stephen feels about it. He feels that the ball is a "greasy leather orb," and that it "flew like a heavy bird through the grey light." In the interests of the realistic and accurate representation of Stephen's youthful experience the novelist must use these words, but equally he cannot possibly have Stephen use such words.

The presence of those two different kinds of language and syntax in the same paragraph simultaneously reinforces our awareness of both the difference and the similarity between the young Stephen and the novelist telling the tale. The method at the outset is omniscient; Stephen himself at the age of six or seven is obviously not telling the story. A novelist is doing so, in fairly conventional fashion. When we add our awareness of this novelist with his conventional manner of narration to the sense of the shaping novelist aroused by the way the first section was told, and then find the narrative moving abruptly back again into Stephen's own language, we are tolerably sure that the novelist telling us the story of *A Portrait* must be Stephen, though when much older. After all, would anyone but Stephen himself possess the telescoped knowledge of the experience of the first section, and could anyone but a novelist—which is to say, an artist—both arrange that material in the order it appears and also describe the football scrimmage in so strikingly formal, so self-consciously and conventionally literary a fashion?

In examining the opening pages of *A Portrait* minutely, there is the danger not only of being too elementary and therefore boring, but also of making it seem as if the reader of *A Portrait* and of other novels must be a trained literary critic, and perhaps a highly tiresome and pedestrian one at that, in order to understand the novel. Of course I mean no such thing. For just as the experience of Stephen at the football scrimmage is much more complex than he would ever think to describe it at the time, so the experience of the reader is more complex than he might at first think. The reader assumes the relationship between the Stephen who is the character and the author who is privy to his thoughts. Part of the function of a passage such as the one describing the football game, in which the author assumes for several sentences the role of conventional, omniscient narrator, and which alone does *not* depend on the reader's awareness of an autobiographical relationship, would appear to be that of *showing* the reader that the older, remembering storyteller who has told us the first section *is* now a *novelist,* a writer. This, at any rate, is its implication for us. Whether the apparently careful juxtaposition is the conscious, premeditated intention of Joyce is not important, either; James Joyce did it, and we read it that way.

The critical argument over the lyric-epic-dramatic passage, it seems to me, arises in part out of a failure to realize the extent to which we read *A Portrait* as autobiographical fiction. Has the author refined himself out of existence, and presented his story objectively? Not if by autobiographical fiction is meant the presence, in the reader's consciousness, of a relationship between Stephen Dedalus the character and the author who is writing the book. For we are quite conscious of this relationship.

Who is this author? Is he James Joyce? My point, once again, is that he is not, however much he may share many of James Joyce's attitudes and much of James Joyce's history. In the first place, not all of Stephen's history as related in *A Portrait* was James Joyce's; biographical research has demonstrated this. More importantly, the autobiographical personality is not a creature of life, but of art. He is as much an artistic product as the youthful Stephen Dedalus, or for that matter as Huckleberry Finn. He is not a character, so much as a static *persona* or focal point of consciousness, created by the author in the act of telling his story. His role is formal, not biographical or historical. He is, as Wayne Booth says, the "implied author," an artistic creation.

If we accept this, we may then see that *A Portrait of the*

Artist as a Young Man is, in intention at least, a dramatic novel in Stephen's use of the term, one in which the real-life author, the biographical creator, is not present at all. It is surely *not*, however, a dramatic novel, again in Stephen's definition of the term, if Stephen meant—I suspect he may have—that in a dramatic novel there is no sense of our being told anything by an author. In that case I would agree with Wayne Booth when he declares that "whether an impersonal novelist hides behind a single narrator or observer, the multiple points of view of *Ulysses* or *As I Lay Dying*, or the objective surfaces of *The Awkward Age* or Compton-Burnett's *Parents and Children*, the author's voice is never really silenced." [6] Surely *A Portrait*, from its opening lines onward, is very much the product of a virtuoso, and we are not allowed to forget it.

What Joyce has done in *A Portrait* and *Ulysses* is to create fiction in which the artist character represents himself when young. What this means about *Ulysses* I shall shortly try to show. For the Portrait it means that the reader, responding to the presence of the "implied author," senses that whatever Stephen Dedalus' difficulties and however callow his youth, eventually Stephen is going to become a novelist. In part, I think, this helps to explain what Booth has noted when he remarks that the earlier critical readings of *A Portrait* tended to take Stephen at face value, without noting the strong irony Joyce uses in describing him. "Those of us," Booth says, "who now believe that Joyce is not entirely serious in the passages on aesthetics must wonder, for example, how we ever read them 'straight.'" [7] Consider the line that directly precedes Stephen's famed statement of genres: "Stephen paused and, though his companion did not speak, felt that his words had called up

6. Wayne Booth, *The Rhetoric of Fiction* (Chicago, 1961), p. 60.
7. *Ibid.*, p. 334, n. 38.

around them a thought enchanted silence." (p. 213) I read that line now and I smile at the irony being directed at Stephen's egocentricity. But why did I not notice it twenty years ago when I first encountered *A Portrait*? In part because I was evidently quite willing to accept Stephen's naïve evaluation of his own importance. But my willingness to accept this was greatly augmented by the legitimate assumption that Stephen stood for the author when younger; he spoke with the authority of being the eventual creator of both *A Portrait* and *Ulysses*.

Was I justified in doing this? I think I was. For Joyce, as I have attempted to demonstrate, had *made me* read *A Portrait* as an autobiographical novel, a novel in which the reader is made to discern a relationship between the "implied author" and the protagonist. And where I went wrong was with the fifth section of *A Portrait*, which I read without perceiving any irony. For Joyce really becomes ironic about Stephen Dedalus' youthful pretensions only in that fifth chapter; up until then the novel not only may be read "straight," as Wayne Booth says, but indeed cannot very well be read any other way. Not even the scene in which Stephen, having renounced a theological vocation, walks out along the sea and discovers profane beauty, is really written tongue in cheek, for all its profane interruptions. The youth who has undergone the torment of the sermons, and then has emerged from his religious vigil, has by then earned the reader's respect; one is quite willing to sympathize with his youthful seriousness, and if at times he seems a bit too intense for one's taste—"Now, as never before, his strange name seemed to him a prophecy" (p. 168)—I merely ascribe this to his youth. After all, he does eventually justify that seriousness by creating the novel we are reading, does he not?

In the final section, however, Joyce stresses the irony. The reader can miss it entirely, and take Stephen at face value. If one's reaction is like my own when I first read the novel at the age of twenty, one will probably continue to see Stephen as Hero, and accept his own evaluation of his importance. If one is unwilling to accept Stephen's romantic sense of mission, however, one is likely to object strenuously to the whole thing, point to his callowness, the absurdity of his esthetic theorizing, and belabor James Joyce for romanticizing Stephen, as indeed many critics did.

The intended response is for the reader to perceive what Joyce is attempting to do with Stephen in the way of irony, in which case one's attitude is likely to be based upon whether or not one thinks Joyce's irony is successful. For myself, I do not think it entirely so, for all that there are some purple passages and cutting phrases sprinkled in among the esthetic theorizing and in that episode in which Stephen writes a very mediocre poem. In the first place, there is too much theorizing and too little commenting on the theorizing. As a piece of exposition the esthetic theory makes perfectly good sense, so far as unity and coherence go; it is presented forcefully and clearly enough to make us, especially considering the length of the scene, read it on its merits and not as characterization. The interjections of Lynch seem only devices to give the interlude the appearance of fiction. It does not seem very good fiction.

At this point the distinction between the "implied author" and the real-life author breaks down. The "implied author" which Joyce has created, the author whose presence we have sensed throughout the first four portions of the novel, perhaps without entirely realizing we have done so, fails; we see James Joyce attempting to fictionalize his youthful esthetic theory by placing it in Stephen's voice, and by a few weak attempts at intervening dialogue—"—Let us take her, said Lynch fervently"—

seeking to give it the appearance of being something other than expository theory. The ironic qualifications are not sufficiently dramatic or extensive to right the balance; there is too much straight theory, not nearly enough sense of Stephen, rather than Joyce, as theorist. (In this respect it is at the opposite remove from the Shakespearean theorizing in *Ulysses*.) As for the objection that the theory is meant to be ironic, coming as it does from Stephen, one can only reply that if so, the irony fails to come across. Not only does the theorizing make considerable sense, but it also fails to contradict, and contrast with, what Stephen Dedalus has come to be—and this despite the fact that Stephen's mode of thinking in abstract categories is dramatically appropriate to his struggle to renounce the particularities of his home, church, and nation in order to become an Artist. What contrast it possesses is intellectual, static; the reader is asked to juxtapose an esthetic theory with a created character. Again, the effect is to make us aware of the presence of James Joyce striving to get his point across; and this is not at all the role Joyce is seeking to convey. The fictional relationship is for the moment crippled. No longer do we have the sense of an authorial persona creating a story, looking back upon himself when young; instead we are all too conscious of the flesh-and-blood James Joyce laboring to give order and meaning to recalcitrant material.

When Stephen writes his villanelle, once again the irony is not enough to make us stand back and cease to take Stephen at face value. For one thing, the poem is *not* all that bad. It is certainly no worse than many of the poems in *Chamber Music*. It is only mediocre, run-of-the-mill verse, which is something else again. That Stephen's method of composing the poem contrasts with his theory of the artist standing back indifferently, paring his fingernails, is true; but the created poem does not conflict with the theory. It is quite "objective," quite "impersonal"; its defects lie elsewhere. One is not at all sure that Joyce means for Stephen to appear comic in the act of writing his poem. If sometimes the language appears purplish, at other times one does not know. Even occasional bits of incongruity—"The earth was like a swinging, swaying censer, a ball of incense, an ellipsoidal ball" (p. 28)—are not keen enough in the aggregate to make us draw back. Again the fictional relationship is in danger. What is James Joyce trying to do here? we ask. Does he realize that Stephen's poem is fairly ordinary? Does he realize that Stephen is striking attitudes, posing? One wonders, and to the extent that one does, the fictional relationship breaks down.

Not until the dialogue with Cranly and the final diary entries does the author again seem fully in control of his young man. Significantly, here the role of authorial irony is not so important, for in the diary Stephen begins for the first time to exercise a little irony upon himself. In these sequences, one can for the most part take Stephen pretty much at face value. The "implied author" is again firmly established; the Stephen who confirms his separation to Cranly, and who makes diary entries as he prepares to leave for the continent, is obviously the younger self of the author who chronicles his story. Only at the end does this separation falter, for me at least; "Welcome, O life! I go to encounter for the millionth time the reality of experience and to forge in the smithy of my soul the uncreated conscience of my race." (p. 253) Is that word "forge" really a pun, in the style of Shem the Penman? No matter; for Stephen Dedalus the artist as a young man, the dramatization, the hyperbole of that manifesto seem appropriate. And if there is any doubt, the humility of the final entry, our realization of what Stephen is about to do, make it seem right and appropriate:

April 27. Old father, old artificer, stand me now and ever in good stead.

Dublin, 1904.
Trieste, 1914. (p. 253)

That Stephen is back in Dublin, with his French artist's cap, teaching at a preparatory school, when we begin *Ulysses*, is enough to get the novel off to a good start. That he is bitter, aloof, withdrawn, is appropriate; nor is there any doubt that this is what the author has in mind. Of the identity of the author there is also no doubt. In the first place there is *A Portrait*, which one has read; we know who Stephen Dedalus is, and we recognize him immediately, and remember the relationship in which he existed to the authorial voice who gave us his story. We apprehend at once the presence of that same authorial voice, describing Buck Mulligan this time:

Halted, he peered down the dark winding stairs and called up coarsely:
—Come up, Kinch. Come up, you fearful Jesuit.
Solemnly he came forward and mounted the round gunrest. He faced about and blessed gravely thrice the tower, the surrounding country and the awaking mountains. . . . (p. 3)

And two pages later when Stephen thinks of a dream about his dead mother, there is no question who the focal character of this episode will be. Buck Mulligan takes Stephen by the arm. "Cranly's arm. His arm," Stephen thinks (p. 7). Same character, same artist looking back and creating him.

But after we follow Stephen to breakfast, then to work, and after that out along the shore, and leave him while the sailing ship goes by, we begin a new section, and we have a new character, Leopold Bloom. The advent of this little man introduces a new element to James Joyce's fiction. For the first time, really, there is straight comedy. There is a non-artist, a non-autobiographical protagonist. That is, there is a great deal of James Joyce in the makeup of Leopold Bloom, but Bloom is not importantly an authorial surrogate, and does not exist in the same causal relationship as Stephen does to the "implied author," the authorial voice. Not only that, but, as we shall see, it is essential to the meaning of *Ulysses* that he not do so.

In depicting both Stephen and Bloom, Joyce makes strong use of what in the *Portrait* he only briefly introduces, the technique of the stream of consciousness. Now the stream of consciousness, designed as it is to illustrate not only what someone is thinking but the way in which he thinks, can be used both to disguise and to inform. The technique is a highly adaptable medium, and of course this is in part because it isn't really the accurate reproduction of thought at all, but a literary representation made to appear like unmediated thought. I stress this point because an important formal relationship in *Ulysses* exists in the several ways that Joyce uses the stream of consciousness. Stephen thinks, Bloom thinks; we see each of them thinking. But, especially during the earlier episodes in the book when Joyce's need to set up his relationships is most crucial, Stephen and Bloom not only think differently about things, but there is an important difference in the way Joyce describes them thinking. In the episode with Mulligan and Haines, even more so with the schoolmaster Mr. Deasy and while walking alone on the shore, the interior monologue that is Stephen's thought is almost exclusively from the inside, as it were; we are made to see *with* Stephen, and then to follow the associations within his mind. Seldom are we told that Stephen *did* this or that, *saw* this or that. Instead we receive the thing seen or done, as Stephen sees or does it. This is not an absolutely consistent practice, perhaps because we might then grow confused, but Joyce tells us what Stephen is doing only often enough not to lose us. Most of the time we see *with* Stephen:

> A bloated carcass of a dog lay lolled on bladder-wrack. Before him the gunwhale of a boat, sunk in sand. *Un coche ensable,* Louis Veuillot called Gautier's prose. These heavy sand are language tide and wind have silted here. . . . (p. 44)

Stephen sees something, and is reminded of a literary allusion, which then reminds him of language, of his own wouldbe vocation as writer, and so on. To be sure, this helps to characterize Stephen, but it also causes us to identify with him as well, to accept his version of his experience. It is approximately the same relationship as in the *Portrait.*

But when Joyce turns to Leopold Bloom, and wants to show us the way he thinks, he is constantly *showing us Bloom,* and then letting us see him think:

> He went out through the backdoor into the garden: stood to listen towards the next garden. No sound. Perhaps hanging clothes out to dry. The maid was in the garden. Fine morning. (p. 68)

Again, this is not an absolutely consistent practice; sometimes several paragraphs elapse before we see Bloom from outside again. But compared with Stephen's monologue, that of Bloom flows much less smoothly from within, and is interrupted with much greater frequency in order that we may look at Bloom. In part this is because Bloom is a much more richly comic character, but that too is significant, for by its very nature comedy precludes identification with a character, and demands that we view the character from outside and above. For the success of the Bloom episodes it is important that our view be from above, so that we see Bloom both as he appears to the others, as he appears to himself, and as he really is. The chapter describing

Paddy Dignam's funeral, for example, is a moving piece of writing. Its success depends in large part on our ability to see the difficulties Bloom has in getting along with his fellow mourners, their relative insensitivity as compared with Bloom's meditations on what he sees, and Bloom's essential decency and kindness. Not only, therefore, does Joyce show us the conversation taking place, and Bloom's frequent (though by no means constant or consistent) inner meditations on what he hears and what it brings up in his mind, but he sometimes breaks away from Bloom entirely in order to allow the other characters to talk about Bloom when he is out of earshot.

Leopold Bloom is a good man, a kind man, a sensitive man, but he is of a limited, however alert, intelligence, and it is important that we perceive his limitations. Stephen Dedalus likewise is limited, but not by his intelligence so much as by his lack of experience. Thus while we may not always agree with Stephen's evaluation of what is going on, *we seldom question the veracity of his report,* and in all but the final scenes in the novel, whenever he is on stage we see with him and identify with him. With Bloom, by contrast, however much we may admire and sympathize with him, we seldom identify with him to the extent of seeing what is going on precisely as he does, and his evaluation of his experience is often not ours or the author's. The meaning, rather, lies in the discrepancy between what Bloom thinks is going on and what actually is happening. This is especially true in the chapters that center upon his monologues. When for example Bloom gives Bantam Lyons the newspaper, it is obvious to us that Bantam sees something going on in the conversation that Bloom doesn't. Much later we learn that by twice repeating the words "throw it away," Bloom has unwittingly given Bantam a tip on the Ascot Gold Cup race. (pp. 85–86) Bloom does not realize this, but the incident helps to dampen his welcome among the habituees at Barney Kiernan's saloon later on. In other chapters, such as the one at Kiernan's in which Joyce has a pub crawler tell what happens in the form of a straightforward monologue and with constant interruptions for parodies of newspaper accounts, histories, chronicles, and the like, Bloom is seen entirely from without. And in the scene after the street brawl, when Bloom takes Stephen in tow, the discrepancy between what Bloom is thinking and saying and what he thinks Stephen is saying, on the one hand, and what we perceive is more probably going on within Stephen's mind on the other, lies at the heart of the episode's meaning.

I have dwelled on this distinction between Bloom's thinking and Stephen's thinking for the reason that it is absolutely vital to the meaning of *Ulysses*. Without it, and what it means, the novel will not make sense. Nothing will "happen."

What does happen in *Ulysses?* What is its "plot"? Most critics, I think correctly, describe it as something like this: Stephen Dedalus, home from an abortive journey to Paris, wanders about the city of Dublin, bitter, proud, alone. Late in the evening he encounters a friend of his father's, a converted Jew named Leopold Bloom, who as an advertising salesman has spent a largely ineffective day about town, worrying at times over the unfaithfulness of his wife Molly. Stephen, drunken, becomes involved in a street brawl, from which Bloom extricates him, conducts him to an all-night restaurant to get him something to eat and drink, then takes him home, where his wife Molly lies asleep upstairs. The now sober Stephen, recognizing the kindness and humanity of Bloom, finds what has hitherto been lacking in his life and what he has been searching for: in Tindall's words, "charity, humanity, maturity, and self. Discovering Bloom ('Everyman or Noman'), Stephen discovers mankind. Joining Bloom, he becomes himself. . . . Given understanding of humanity by Bloom's humanity, no longer separated by pride and childish ego from every other man, Stephen sees himself as everyman, himself grown up." [8] And when Bloom and Stephen stand outside in the dark below Molly's lighted window, to quote Tindall again, "Stephen is able to share Bloom's vision. Understanding Bloom has prepared the way for the fundamental and more charitable understanding that Molly demands. What Stephen apprehends is revealed in the next chapter. Knowing Bloom and Molly, as every writer must, Stephen knows humanity entirely. Let him go away now and write about it." [9]

This account is I think largely justified. But an important question must here be asked. *How do we know that this is what happened?* The physical peregrinations of Stephen and Bloom we have witnessed, but what is the authority for assuming that Bloom holds the meaning for Stephen that Tindall says he does? On what authority can one say that the Molly Bloom soliloquy which ends *Ulysses* is "what Stephen apprehends"? How do we know that "Stephen knows humanity entirely" at the end of the novel? Unless I am mistaken, almost nothing in what Joyce has shown of Stephen's thoughts in any way reveals this. He does, it is true, look at Bloom at one point and think, *"Christus or Bloom his name is, or, after all, any other, secundum carnem."* (p. 643) But to read into this one passing thought the intense revelation of humanity and vocation that supposedly comes to Stephen while in Bloom's company is scarcely justifiable. Nor does the Homeric parallel, suggested by the novel's title and by certain references and allusions scattered throughout the book, seem reason enough for such a dramatic conclusion; if

8. W. Y. Tindall, *A Reader's Guide to James Joyce* (New York, 1959), p. 222.

9. *Ibid.*, pp. 224–25.

Bloom is Odysseus and Stephen Telemachus, then why does the son go away at the end? The Homeric parallel can be only a very general frame for Joyce's novel, and imposed as it is from without, it is a thin structure upon which to build this important development.

The appropriateness of such an interpretation of *Ulysses* depends not only on the actions and thoughts of the characters, but also upon our realization of the formal relationship between Stephen Dedalus and the author of *Ulysses*. For unless we know that Stephen wrote the book, that the book itself is the ultimate product of his meeting with Bloom, we have little warrant for assuming any of the meaning which Tindall and most other good critics ascribe to what happens in the novel. The obvious fact that an older Stephen could create the characters of Leopold Bloom and his wife Molly is the only proof we have for this conclusion.[10]

10. I confess that I wrote this chapter before coming upon Stanley Sultan's brilliant reading of Joyce's novel (*The Argument of Ulysses* [Columbus, Ohio, 1964]). By giving Joyce's book a closer reading than anyone had ever done before, Mr. Sultan has been able to recognize and to present in convincing fashion a much more detailed and specific "plot" line than had hitherto been assumed, especially in reference to Leopold Bloom's Homeric odyssey. Though this does not make the role of the authorial personality may less valuable to the reading of the novel, it does indicate, and unmistakably, that considerably more "plot" is present in the book's texture than anyone had thought.

Yet this in turn raises a problem. If Joyce *intended* for the reader to be able to grasp what Mr. Sultan demonstrates about the plot, then one would have to admit that even for the "ideal reader suffering from the ideal insomnia," Joyce made things awfully difficult. For unfortunately, so much of the material on which Mr. Sultan bases his excellent analysis is present in the novel only in very static form indeed.

Mr. Sultan's book is full of perceptive and original observations about *Ulysses* and *A Portrait*. At one point he contends that the portrait of Stephen as the young artist is drawn from life, but not from Joyce's life; it is rather that of Joyce's brother Stanislaus. James Joyce as a youth was

But we do know that he wrote the book, and therefore ample proof. We know it because of the relationship we have long since perceived between Stephen and the "implied author." This is why I have emphasized the difference in the way Joyce writes about Stephen and about Bloom. We sympathize with Bloom, but we identify with Stephen. Thus we grant to Stephen the range of imagination and insight necessary, when more mature, to compose the book, and we recognize his relationship

far too good-spirited, robust, high-hearted to serve as model for the gloomy, lonely, alienated Stephen Dedalus; but from all that is known of Stanislaus, he fits the model quite well. This is why Stephen's brother Maurice, in *Stephen Hero,* was left out of *A Portrait,* Mr. Sultan speculates; he had been transformed into the central character.

It is an ingenious theory, but I do not think it is valid. The important thing is that Stephen Dedalus is the *artist;* and such a role simply does not fit Stanislaus as his brother saw him. Mr. Sultan thinks that Stephen's specifically artistic characteristics are drawn from the autobiography of James Mangan, and from Hauptmann's Michael Kramer. But I believe that although Stephen is not in every detail a self-portrait, the essential characteristics were patterned after James Joyce's conception of himself when young. Surely almost everything that Stephen does or thinks has its counterpart in James Joyce's career as a youth; Richard Ellmann demonstrates this in considerable detail. To be sure, there is little of "Sunny Jim" Joyce, as his brother and friends remembered him, in Stephen, insofar as the youthful Joyce's good humor, insouciance, and robustness are involved. But what author of an artistic "bildungsroman" such as *A Portrait* has ever portrayed his youthful self in that fashion? One need only consult such novels as *Remembrance of Things Past, The Way of All Flesh, This Side of Paradise,* and *Look Homeward, Angel,* and compare the protagonists of those novels to the youthful personalities of their authors, as remembered by friends and acquaintances, to see that in such novels a transformation apparently is standard procedure. It would seem that however outgoing, gregarious, light-hearted the authors of this kind of novel may have seemed to others when young, they do not think of themselves as ever having been that kind of person. They seem to remember themselves mostly as lonely and alienated young men, whatever others who knew them may have thought. There can be little doubt, I feel, that when James Joyce created the character of Stephen Dedalus, it was of his own youthful self that he was chiefly thinking—which is not to say, of course, that Joyce did not use much material that was not drawn specifically from his own life in developing his protagonist. But in the main, Stephen is taken from life: his creator's life.

to the implied author telling the story. The book's meaning absolutely depends upon our awareness of the presence of an "implied author," a transcendent artistic voice linked causally to one of the characters. Stephen has within him the potentiality to become that author. Bloom has not, and must not have; he must be limited and incapable of ever being that author: his function is to let us realize that an older, wiser author can create such a person as Bloom. And the same is true, though less importantly, of Molly. We must, by seeing things with as well as through Stephen's eyes, realize what he will some day be able to do, and equally we must, by seeing Dublin through Bloom's eyes and by seeing Bloom in Dublin, realize that he is not and cannot ever become the author of a novel.

There is, of course, a great deal of Bloom in the makeup of James Joyce, and vice versa. As Lenahan admits, "He's a cultured allround man, Bloom is. . . . He's not one of your common or garden . . . you know . . . There's a touch of the artist about old Bloom." (p. 235) But primarily insofar as there is a great deal of everyman in every artist, I think; anyone familiar with Richard Ellmann's excellent biography of Joyce can recognize the relationship between Bloom and his creator, but the relationship is more biographical than formal. Joyce has purposely kept Bloom at a remove; he is the antithesis of the Godlike creative artist (he may well be the Christlike sufferer, but that is another matter). Joyce's affection for Bloom is mingled with a certain amount of contempt, too. But for the meaning of *Ulysses* the important thing to realize is that Bloom, though he live to be a thousand years old, could never have written *Stephen Hero*, let alone *Ulysses*. We know this, and we know that Stephen Dedalus on the other hand could and probably did write both. Stephen, and not Bloom, is the autobiographical character, if by that term is meant the character whose experience, and equally as important, whose frame of mind and whose sensitivity, are like the authorial personality's own, and who can thus grow into that "implied author" who plays so prominent a part in *Ulysses*.

Which brings us, by a commodius vicus of recirculation, back to the good ship *Rosevean*, Dublin-bound with a cargo of bricks. Stephen sees the vessel, silently moving homeward, as he too turns toward Dublin. Haines and Mulligan do not see it, but it is there, and we see it—immediately following the hint given us that Stephen will write something "in ten years." (p. 249) The mariner comes home. The artist reaches manhood, discovers his own humanity. And in a thousand ways he calls attention to himself, to the fact that he created all this, throughout the novel. Symbols; puns; daring and self-conscious techniques; a fugal chapter in which first we are given two pages of sounds in the form of words, and then find all those sounds worked into the events of the narrative that follows; parodies—if ever there was a highly visible artist, it is the novelist who wrote *Ulysses*. And in the Library episode, Stephen expounds a theory of *Hamlet* and Shakespeare that sets forth the whole relationship—obliquely, as if to contrast with Stephen the theorizer of *A Portrait*. If Hamlet is Shakespeare's son Hamnet, then the ghost of the dead king is Shakespeare; the artist creates his son, to avenge his own murder and cuckoldry; Bloom is ghostly father to Stephen, but Stephen is creator of himself, prince when young and ghostly king grown old: "He is a ghost, a shadow now, the wind by Elsinore's rocks or what you will, the sea's voice, a voice heard only in the heart of him who is the substance of his shadow, the son consubstantial with the father." (p. 197) As the successive episodes of *Ulysses* reveal themselves, the authorial personality draws away from his characters, and in Olympian fashion recapitulates their lives and destinies from "behind or above his handiwork"—but he is not invisible, refined out of existence, paring his fingernails in aloof indifference. For *Ulysses* is a comic novel, and the joy is for the artist as well as the reader.

The artist is not always successful. In a chapter such as the "Oxen of the Sun," for example, in which Bloom visits the Lying-in Hospital to see how Mrs. Purefoy is doing, and takes up with the medical students in order to look after Stephen, the birth of Mrs. Purefoy's baby is recapitulated in the birth of the language, and there are a series of parodies which amuse few and confuse many readers. Nor am I convinced that the famous Nighttown episode, in which we see all through the merging somnambulatory hallucinations of Bloom and Stephen, does its job in the best manner possible, and this in spite of the combined efforts of Mr. Tindall, Mr. Stanley Sultan, Mr. S. L. Goldberg, and others to coach me in what is going on. In these chapters, as in Stephen's disquisition on esthetics in *A Portrait*, it is no longer the authorial personality who is addressing me; it is James Joyce with his "true scholastic stink," laboring to be funny or profound. An immense difficulty with Joyce is that throughout his literary life he never fully apprehended the difference between static and dynamic use of symbol and theory; much of the placing of symbols and leitmotifs in *Ulysses* is static, inert, meaning little or nothing about what is going on. Let it never be forgotten that the author of *Ulysses* and *A Portrait* is the author of *Finnegans Wake*. There are points in which *Ulysses* comes close to the inert, symbol-laden and pun-bedecked mass of the sleeping giant of Howth Castle and environs. . . . "that master manufacturer of literary cuckoo-clocks," one unkind critic has called Joyce.[11]

11. Karl Shapiro, *In Defense of Ignorance* (New York, 1960), p. 247.

Joyce is a great writer not in the profundity of his esthetic theorizing, not in the skill of his parodying, not even—though here one is less sure—in the wild genius of his symbol-making, but in his tremendous capacity for self-revelation, for the creation of characters. He dramatized himself, and he saw himself in others and he dramatized that. "Local colour. Work in all you know." Can one ever forget the rich, flowering excitement of Dublin, June 16, 1904? And the excitement is sustained because it works out to *mean* something—to Stephen, to the author, and so to us. We see it happen. The development of *Ulysses* is that of seeing the city, the universe, life itself and his own relationship to it, come into focus for the artistic personality Stephen Dedalus became, as related to us by that personality. "The events of the book," S. L. Goldberg points out in his excellent analysis of *Ulysses*, "point toward the act by which the events themselves will finally be understood—an act completed by the 'mythic' vision of the last episodes. In *formal* terms apart from the represented *events*, the author's understanding pervades the whole book, unobtrusively arranging and informing the material; but so important a character requires a more noticeable part. Delicately, tactfully, the author must draw attention to himself as outside the represented events." [12] And again:

Not only does *Ulysses* become, in one aspect, a symbolistic "drama of meaning," but since it is also a drama about its own birth, it necessarily includes, as Stephen's argument [about Shakespeare] unmistakably suggests, a hidden character: *the author himself.* He is not the real Joyce, of course—the Joyce who was known to his friends and died in 1941; not a mere *persona* either; but Joyce the artistic or poetic personality

12. S. L. Goldberg, *The Classical Temper: A Study of James Joyce's "Ulysses"* (London, 1961), p. 36.

whose voice has completely passed into his work. In *Ulysses* he lives in his characters, but beyond them.[13]

The same is true of *A Portrait*. It should be remembered that if Stephen Dedalus is leaving No. 7 Eccles Street to go forth and create his art, it is not *Ulysses* he will create, but *A Portrait of the Artist as a Young Man*. That is the book that bears the ten-year date, "Dublin, 1904, Trieste, 1914." That is the book that comes closer to what Stephen as we last see him may soon be able to write. Leopold and Molly Bloom must wait their turn.

Stephen Dedalus, the future artist in *A Portrait*, sets for himself this question: "Is the bust of Sir Philip Crampton lyrical, epical or dramatic? If not, why not?" (p. 214) In *Ulysses* Leopold Bloom, riding toward Paddy Dignam's funeral, looks out the window of the carriage. "Sir Philip Crampton's memorial fountain bust," he thinks. And he adds, "Who was he?" (p. 92)

In the difference between these two questions, we could well say, lies the meaning of the discovery of artistic vocation that is the true subject of James Joyce's two great novels.

13. *Ibid.*, p. 35.

SEVEN · François Mauriac; or,
The Novelist as Theologian

T HERE is one kind of novel about which little has thus far
been said in this study, but that very much belongs in any
consideration of the role of the novelist within his novel. It is the
so-called religious novel, of which François Mauriac is perhaps
the leading practitioner in our time. In this kind of novel, the
author's intention—consciously, at any rate—is not simply to
explore the meaning of a human situation, but also to interpret
that situation in the light of a preconceived, revealed body of
meaning. The problems involved thereby are fairly obvious, and
have been argued by critics and estheticians more learned than
myself. From the point of view of this study, however, they
come down to this: when a novelist knows in advance what the
meaning of his story should be, how does this affect his status
as storyteller? Can he, should he avoid becoming, or seeming
to become, a theologian rather than a novelist? Can the authorial personality who tells the story thrive in such a role?
What, in short, is the function, if any, of the "implied author"
of a religious novel?

We have had religious novelists in America, some of them
Catholics; and some of them, including Katherine Anne Porter
and Flannery O'Connor, have been distinguished writers. But in
the work of none of them, it seems to me, does the question of
religion and literature, or more properly religion *in* literature,
present quite the same formal problems as in François Mauriac's
best work. The nearest thing to Mauriac over here, I think, is a

novel written not by a Catholic but by a Protestant, Nathaniel Hawthorne's *The Scarlet Letter*.

At first glance this may seem odd, but not if one considers Mauriac's particular brand of Roman Catholicism. For Mauriac's Catholicism is heavily Jansenist. Not for nothing does he still keep his childhood edition of the *Pensées* at his side. "The fire of one night of Pascal," he tells us in a recent essay, "was sufficient to illuminate our entire life, and like the child whom the night light reassures in his room full of shadows, because of that fire we are not afraid to go to sleep" [1] (Note, in passing, the Proustian metaphor.) Pascal's famous remark, reported often by Mauriac, that "marriage is the lowest of all Christian states, vile and unpleasing to God," lies, in a curious and from both a theological and a psychological standpoint a quite fascinating way, at the heart of Mauriac's art. The Catholicism of Pascal, and of Mauriac, is much closer to Calvinism than to the Catholicism of, say, a Jacques Maritain or a Roger Martin du Gard. Mauriac is a Puritan—much more so in fact than Nathaniel Hawthorne, for whom the Calvinist God of his forebears had been considerably diluted by generations of the Enlightenment and by the intoxicating Transcendentalism that was being brewed all about him in New England. Mauriac takes sin very gravely, and his view of the human condition is aptly characterized in his foreword to *Thérèse Desqueyroux* when he refers to "the secrets of the hearts that are deep buried in, and mingled with, the filth of flesh." [2]

It is very difficult for most modern readers to believe in "the filth of flesh." Nor can Mauriac as novelist be said to believe it

1. François Mauriac, *What I Believe*, trans. Wallace Fowlie (New York, 1963), p. 113.
2. François Mauriac, *Thérèse: A Portrait in Four Parts*, trans. Gerard Hopkins (New York, 1964), p. 4.

himself, in an important sense. But both Mauriac and Hawthorne can take the conflict of flesh and spirit with absolute
seriousness, so that the conflicting claims of body and soul can
become for both of them the material of human tragedy. Most
of us probably do not really believe that the body exists in
opposition to the soul. If this seems an extreme statement, consider this test. When in *A Portrait of the Artist as a Young Man*
young Stephen Dedalus visits Nighttown at an early age, how
many of us consider this action impure? Rather, we are interested in its psychological impact on Stephen, its role in bringing
to a head the religious experience of the retreat sequence. Another example: in *Light in August* Faulkner remarks of Joe
Christmas that "his own life, for all its anonymous promiscuity,
had been conventional enough, as a life of healthy and normal
sin usually is." [3] How many of us find that a shocking statement?
Yet from a Calvinistic point of view what is sinful can in no
way be healthy; and Faulkner's statement would be as heretical
a remark as could be made.

Whatever we may profess to believe, we do not, in short,
really consider casual sexual relationships invariably sinful. On
the contrary, it is repression, when carried past normal human
endurance, that we consider psychologically unhealthy. Thus
when we read *The Scarlet Letter* it is difficult for us to see Hester
Prynne's and Arthur Dimmesdale's sin as being against God.
Their act is a sin against the laws of society, and while we may
not approve of what Hester and the Reverend Dimmesdale did,
we consider it understandable, given the weakness of the flesh.
But Hawthorne, with the heritage of his Puritan ancestry, was
able to take Hester's and Dimmesdale's violation of the marriage
law and of the Seventh Commandment with sufficient serious-

3. William Faulkner, *Light in August* (New York, 1950), p. 227.

ness to play off the sense of moral crime against human need and desire so as to create tragedy.

Precisely the same kind of problem arises in Mauriac's best work. Now Mauriac shares none of Hawthorne's occasional optimism. He could never approve of a character's predicting, as Hester does, that "at some brighter period, when the world should have grown ripe for it, in Heaven's own time, a new truth would be revealed, in order to establish the whole relation between man and woman on a surer ground of mutual happiness." [4] Intellectually, Mauriac's Jansenist position would be much closer to that of the Puritans. But emotionally, humanly, Mauriac is drawn toward sinners, and in his very denunciation of sin, in the lurid colors he uses to paint it, he reveals the attraction it holds for him. (Hawthorne's emotional involvement, by contrast, was in a very real sense with the Calvinist attitude, while intellectually he inclined toward the optimistic view.)

The point is that in Mauriac, as in Hawthorne, one encounters this dramatic tension between a puritanical view of the flesh and a passionate sympathy with the human position. The divided nature of the human being is thus dramatized, and the problem grows out of social and psychological terms into those involving the religious nature of man. But because Mauriac's attitude toward the sins of the flesh is heavily charged with emotion, and because, I think, his Jansenist attitude clashes sharply with his identity in a modern world which is not very Jansenist and puritanical, his novels possess abundantly what is missing in Hawthorne: the heavy sensuousness, even sensuality, of the physical existence, the lure of the body that safeguards them from being what puritanical literature is always in danger

---

4. Nathaniel Hawthorne, *The Scarlet Letter*, eds. E. Sculley Bradley, R. C. Beatty, and E. Hudson Long, Norton Critical ed. (New York, 1962), p. 186.

of being, thin and bodiless allegory. (Which is not to say that
I think Mauriac as good a novelist as Hawthorne; I don't.)

One of Mauriac's best novels is *Lines of Life*. In it, a widow,
Elisabeth Gormac, realizes only after she has recoiled in horror
from a clumsy attempt at lovemaking by a drunken neighbor,
Bob Lagave, and only after Bob has subsequently been killed
in an automobile accident, that she has indeed been in love with
that dissipated young man. Mauriac says of Elisabeth Gornac
after she gets over her grief and moves back into her widowly
routine of managing the family properties that she "had again
become one of those dead who are carried down the stream of
life." [5]

Let us make sure we understand what he means by "life." It
is true that as a novelist Mauriac has only scorn for those who
go through life without emotional involvement; his handling of
the wealthy, property-minded bourgeoisie of the Landes country is scathing. But he views Elisabeth's one abortive adventure
with grand passion as tragic not only because it was hopeless
and unrequited, but also because it was never anything other
than a human, carnal passion. Had it been consummated, she
would ultimately have been just as badly off, because it would
have been sinful in its very carnality. What could have saved
Elisabeth Gornac, kept her from being one of the dead, was not
requited human passion, but God's Grace. Since God was utterly missing from her life, her fate was sealed. Thus for Mauriac "life" may be preferable to a state of living death, but it
is by no means a sufficient condition. Mauriac views Elisabeth
as a lost soul not merely because society has condemned her to
an existence without love, but because, being human, she did
what humans who want to live must do unless touched by

5. François Mauriac, *Lines of Life*, trans. Gerard Hopkins (New York,
1947), p. 153.

Grace—she sought fulfillment in carnal love. Had she *not* fallen in love with her young neighbor Bob Lagave, in her loveless, emotion-stifled routine she would still have been a lost soul. The most she could expect, one assumes, is a different circle in Hell.

Mauriac's very Jansenist view of the human condition goes something like this. Most human beings live lives of unthinking, animalistic worthlessness, blindly preoccupied with the gross and materialistic concerns of the world. Some human beings break out of this routine and desire something more, which takes the form of a grand passion. These humans are at least "alive"—but like Dante's Paolo and Francesca they are sinners and Hell is their inevitable portion. Only those few fortunate human beings who are gifted with the talent for experiencing God's Grace can triumph over life, but of themselves they can do nothing to merit this Grace.

Of what is generally considered Mauriac's major work, only one novel involves a major development of redemption through Grace. In *Viper's Tangle* the miserly and unhappy Louis, having failed in his attempt to disinherit his family, is eventually overcome by a realization of the futility and deprivation of hatred, and of the joy and beauty of love, and as he dies he writes in his journal words of faith and adoration which have become available to him at last.

Martin Turnell, who has written an excellent essay on Mauriac in *The Art of French Fiction*, finds the tone of this novel exaggerated and the situation essentially false, and declares that it represents the moment in Mauriac's development as an artist in which his Jansenist doctrinal concerns begin imposing themselves too rigidly on his fiction to permit the achievement of believable characterization.[6] While I do not share Turnell's esti-

6. Martin Turnell, *The Art of French Fiction* (London, 1959), pp. 344–47.

mate of the novel, which seems to me to be quite convincing both in the central characterization and in the various episodes, it is quite true, I think, that none of Mauriac's subsequent fiction comes up to the standard of *Viper's Tangle* or most of the novels preceding it, and one reason, I feel, is just this business of the literary uses of Grace.

The problem involved is the whole question of the relation of religion and literature (and by implication, the relation between any externally held system of values and the work of art supposedly embodying them.) From the Jansenist point of view, Grace is something that cannot be earned by works. It is bestowed by God, and the good life is the outward sign of the individual's having been given the capacity for achieving salvation. The position of course is very close to orthodox Calvinism (Rayner Heppenstall declares that Mauriac is "in many respects a Protestant at heart" [7]); it comes right up against the problem of Predestination versus Free Will, and if Jansenist theology does not quite encompass the notion of the Elect, it is nevertheless based on the premise that the human being is "free" only to choose a life of austerity, close to God, and that the Christian's eagerness to live this life constitutes an assurance of his having been selected for salvation. If the human being does *not* choose to live such a life, the presumption is that he has not the God-given ability to do so. This is certainly very close to Election, and it is no wonder that the writings of Blaise Pascal are considered heretical by many Roman Catholics.

What, however, of the psychology of the novelist who would create his fiction from the Jansenist, or for that matter the Calvinist, viewpoint of the nature of man? In one sense, the paths along which his protagonists must travel are set ahead of time; if Grace is to be experienced, surely the possibility of this must

7. Rayner Heppenstall, *The Double Image* (London, 1947), p. 117.

be prepared for in advance. The novelist cannot after all take the role of spectator, and merely record the character's progress as the free working of the imagination dictates, because for the character to achieve salvation, he must be made ready for it, since that is the mark of God's Grace. I cannot see how the novelist can escape the suspicion at least of this foreknowledge. Thus in order to give suspense to his narrative, he is placed in the role of manipulator, a situation filled with peril for the work of literature. For whatever the theological attitudes of the novelist, the novel must give the *appearance* of freedom for its characters. The demands of fictional verisimilitude are such that any sense of the character's being arbitrarily manipulated by the author toward a predetermined result will destroy the experience of the work of literature. Yet if the author does not manipulate, which is to say if he fails to negotiate his character through a reasonably complex fate, how is he to develop his character? The dilemma would seem to be that of either creating static characters, oversimplified and wooden, or taking the characters through a calculated maze of situation, in which case the reader is likely to become conscious of what is going on, and the artistic illusion will be destroyed.

This in part is what Jean-Paul Sartre meant when he objected to Mauriac's *The End of the Night* on the grounds noted earlier, that Mauriac "has chosen divine omniscience and omnipotence. But novels are written *by* men and *for* men. In the eyes of God, Who cuts through appearances and goes beyond them, there is no novel, there is no art, for art thrives on appearances. God," Sartre concluded, "is not an artist. Neither is M. Mauriac." [8] Mauriac had intruded his own presence into the narrative, Sartre felt, and had thus destroyed the fiction. Turnell's

8. Jean Paul Sartre, "François Mauriac and Freedom," in *Literary and Philosophical* Essays, trans. Annette Michelson (New York, 1955), p. 23.

objection to *Viper's Tangle*, previously mentioned, is another way of expressing the same criticism.

Sartre's complaint that Mauriac "has chosen divine omniscience" in telling a story, a complaint I do not think justified with the better novels, points up another danger for the religious novelist. Sartre objects to Mauriac's habit of addressing the reader directly, instead of maintaining the anonymity of the objective work of fiction. Indeed, Mauriac does quite often speak directly to the reader and comment on his character's situation; this is very much a characteristic of his art. For example, at the end of one of the better novels, *The Desert of Love*, an old man waits for his train to leave, and talks with his son who has come to see him off: "To all these questions the doctor replied, 'Yes, yes.' Hungrily he fixed his eyes on the young man who had asked them; the man who was so different from himself, and yet so like him—the part of his own flesh and blood that would survive him for a few more years, but that he was fated never to see again." [9] Obviously the novelist, and not the father or the son in the novel, provides that last decisive bit of information. And often Mauriac goes farther even than this; not only does he intrude his authorial personality, but he points out the moral of what is taking place. Thus in *Lines of Life* he describes Elisabeth Gornac's son Pierre as he thinks about the death of Bob Lagave: "The practical good sense of those who are addicted to the spiritual life led Pierre to turn this discovery to account, to transform it into food for his humility. It is so difficult for the Christian not to think that he is better than other men!" [10] True, and it is also difficult for the Christian novelist to resist pointing it out.

9. François Mauriac, *The Desert of Love*, trans. Gerard Hopkins, Bantam Books ed. (New York, 1960), p. 138.
10. *Lines of Life*, p. 130.

This too, it seems to me, is in part related to Mauriac's Jansenist outlook. For the kind of novelist, I feel, who knows the ultimate fate of his characters before he begins his story, and who designs his story to embody a religious truth ("I am a writer, Lord, and You are the subject of my book," Mauriac has written[11]), moralizing is an occupational hazard. He is, after all, working out his stories with the ultimate verdict already theologically determined; the result is preordained.[12] There is thus every temptation to comment on the meaning of what is being dramatized, since the events are designed to convey this meaning.

But this objection to Mauriac, raised by Sartre, Claude-Edmond Magny and others, is not quite to the point. As Philip Stratford indicates in *Faith and Fiction: Creative Process in Greene and Mauriac,* Sartre is here invoking the principle, which is essentially post-Flaubertian, of the disappearing author, and which is widely accepted nowadays.[13] But the whole affair is more complex than that; it is not only improbable that the author ever quite "disappears" from the reader's consciousness in the way in which some critics would demand, but it is also questionable whether that is really desirable. The rhetorical posture of the novel, as I have sought to show, involves the authorial personality serving as vantage point for what is going on, and part of our "experience" of the work of fiction involves our relationship with the authorial personality, whether or not he ever addresses himself directly to us. The truth, I think, is that one cannot make such pronouncements as Sartre's except in terms of an individual novel. It is not authorial intrusion that

11. *What I Believe,* p. 127.

12. Philip Stratford, *Faith and Fiction: Creative Process in Greene and Mauriac* (South Bend, Ind., 1964), p. 204.

13. *Ibid.,* p. 225.

wrecks a novel, but such intrusion at the expense of the story-telling relationship upon which the novel must depend. And objections such as Sartre's too often fail to take into account the dynamics of fiction, which is not a wooden, cut-and-dried affair.

Turnell's criticism of *Viper's Tangle* is more appropriate; he objects not to the presence of the authorial personality as part of the form of the novel, but to the sense of manipulation, the substitution of external, authorial rhetoric for convincing motivation on the character's part.[14] I do not agree. To my way of thinking, in *Viper's Tangle* as well as in *Lines of Life, Genetrix, A Kiss for the Leper, Thérèse Desqueyroux,* and (to a somewhat less successful degree, I think) *The Desert of Love,* the presence of an authorial personality telling the story is both apprehended and appreciated. A dramatic perspective is set up, a vantage point from which we can watch the events being chronicled.

To return to the question of the religious novel, which is to say, to the question of the relationship between Mauriac's Jansenist principles and their embodiment in fiction, I have noted that only in one of the best novels does the protagonist achieve salvation through Grace. Obviously this salvation, and the road to it, raises fictional problems, because to quote Sartre, "art thrives on appearances," while religion sees through appearances into the reality hidden from men. When Sartre said that "God is not an artist" he was on fairly secure ground. But when he added that neither was François Mauriac an artist, he begged the issue. Assuredly Mauriac is not God, however much he too may create his fictional worlds. For the fictional world, whether Mauriac's, Sartre's, or anyone else's, is one of images; and since the novelist isn't divine, his is a world created in a human image,

14. *The Art of French Fiction,* p. 346.

which means one that deals with human beings and is informed by the insight of the human being who has created it. Mauriac's novels may involve much authorial omniscience, may be constructed with a religious purpose in view, may be filled with moralizing and authorial commentary, but all this is a very human business, and not an activity of divinity.

When, therefore, Mauriac writes a novel, he must deal with Appearances. And that Jansenist disposition of his seems to involve an attribute one comes to associate with other self-conscious moralists, whether in fiction or in everyday life: a savage delight in the sinful fleshiness of the world of men, a highly enthusiastic savoring of corruption—even while castigating it.

The truth of the matter is that François Mauriac is one of the most sensual novelists who has ever practiced the art of fiction. He revels in the senses, even while he attacks their carnality. (Jansenism, Martin Turnell says, is not so much a philosophy or a theology as an emotion.[15]) Mauriac's own Jansenism, with its intensely ascetic attitude toward sin, is placed in a fascinating opposition to Mauriac's sensuality, and the dialectic between the two produces in his best work a highly dramatic tension between soul and body, between God and the ungodly. A most revealing statement appears in Mauriac's recent credo, *What I Believe*, when he writes about "The Demands of Purity." Discussing the psychological complexes of a provincial youth's exposure to a puritanical code that ignored the cravings of the senses, he remarks that "we had to live united with a wild beast whom it was important not to know," and he declares that while for the average youth the code was simply ignored, "the consequences were serious for oversensitive boys. For certain types, repressions and complexes are very serious. They can be

15. *Ibid.*

of great use in the formation of what is called a Catholic novelist, and enrich a successful career as writer. God alone knows what it actually cost the beneficiary." [16]

In these statements, the Augustinian origins of Jansenism are very much in evidence. Were Mauriac to have written "To Paris then I came, where a cauldron of unholy lusts consumed me," one would not be greatly surprised. And Mauriac's statement that "Christian marriage, no matter how much affection joins the couple, is not a remedy against lust" [17] is surely of a kind with Paul's grudging admission that one is better off marrying than burning; or Pascal's statement, quoted earlier, that "marriage is the lowest of all Christian states, vile and unpleasing to God." For Mauriac, the body is in constant opposition to the spirit; and as a novelist Mauriac is drawn to both protagonists. There is nothing serene in Mauriac's Christianity; he feels it assailed on every side by the demands of the world and the flesh, and when he remarked that "above all, we should not scorn the flesh," he means that it is something to be triumphed over, and not to be accepted. Well might Mauriac speak, therefore, of the Drama of Salvation.

One of Mauriac's finest novels, I think, is *A Kiss for the Leper*. It is a marvelously gripping novel because of its tremendous passion, its stunningly dramatic tension between spirit and flesh, between duty and desire. The novel is the story of poor Jean Péloueyre, a repellantly ugly young man of wealthy parents, who is married by his father to a beautiful young woman, Noemie d'Artiailh, daughter of an impoverished but aristocratic family. Martin Turnell notes Mauriac's talent for cruelty and violence in setting up the situation. The single para-

16. *What I Believe*, pp. 48–49.
17. *Ibid.*, pp. 54–55.

graph in which Mauriac describes the young couple's wedding night is, I think, one of the most revulsive descriptions of the marital bed ever composed:

> The bedroom of the boarding house at Arcachon was furnished in sham bamboo. There was no curtain to hide the appliances under the wash basin, and the wallpaper was smeared with squashed mosquitoes. Through the open window the breeze from the port smelled of fish, seaweed and salt. The purr of a motor faded away in the direction of the harbor channel. In the cretonne curtains the curtains of two guardian angels veiled their faces in shame. Jean Péloueyre had a long struggle first against his mirror, then against a dead woman. At dawn a feeble moan marked the end of a battle which had lasted six hours. Drenched in sweat, Jean Péloueyre dared not move,—more hideous than a worm beside the corpse he had at last abandoned.[18]

Prince Hamlet's celebrated remark concerning his mother's bed linen is no more disgusting than that; we realize what Mauriac means when he says that he seeks in his fiction "to render the Catholic universe of evil in terms of sight, touch and smell"! How he seems to revel in the denial of the flesh, to gloat in the misery of that perspiration-drenched bed of toil!

A Kiss for the Leper is a novel of renunciation, what it costs, what it demands. Almost gleefully Mauriac chronicles the terrible bargain whereby two innocents, Jean and Noemie, are sacrificed to their parent's greed. Jean Péloueyre, unloved and unlovely, sins weakly in that he agrees to marry a beautiful woman, with the vague hope that in possessing her he will thereby be transformed and become the Man of Substance that he is not. For this transgression—and Mauriac obviously both loathes and relishes violation of physical beauty by ugliness—Jean pays in mortification, guilt, and despair. Finally, in order to free his

---

18. François Mauriac, *A Kiss for the Leper,* trans. Gerard Hopkins (London, 1950), p. 43.

wife, he seeks out death by repeatedly visiting a tubercular neighbor, until he contracts the disease.

Noemie's ordeal is equally severe; beautiful, full of life, she beds with a man she cannot love or desire, whom all her emotions would lead her to reject. Not by word or conscious deed does she cause Jean to feel more remorseful than he already is. Yet she cannot hide her joy over his imminent departure for Paris to do some research work. Briefly she meets a young doctor and desires him, but she resists her impulses. When Jean returns and slowly dwindles toward death, she is overcome by remorse because she cannot desire him, and she does indeed come to love him—but not as her husband, so much as her victim. Afterward she enters into continued mourning, and when an opportunity comes for her to go to the young doctor, she runs from it.

It is the denial of life by the living; the villain is not really the avaricious parents, but the human condition. Mauriac's picture of Jean Péloueyre is loathsome; mixed with his pity for the plight of the poor unlovely fellow is a savage fascination with the corruption implicit in that ugliness. And his only solution for the absolute impasse between human aspirations and physical loathing is a desperate Jansenist purification of the soul through the sloughing off of the body, the subliming away of the criminal flesh itself.

Nothing could be less austere than Mauriac's attitude toward such matters, and here the lie is given to Sartre's accusation that Mauriac presumes to take a godlike omniscience toward his characters. This novel, in which compassion is inextricably mixed up with contempt, is the very embodiment in human images of that conflict between appearances and reality which Sartre says constitutes the novelist's art. Such Grace as may be possible to poor Noemie d'Artiailh Péloueyre comes only through a bleak shriveling away of all human loveliness. Between Mauriac the sensualist and Mauriac the Jansenist ascetic there evolves a debate between body and soul, between appearance and reality, that attains a tragic and passionate resolution.

As readers, we participate in the debate, because Mauriac is presenting it to us as the struggle he envisions it. He tells us his story, in other words, not from an Olympian distance, far above the struggle, but as a passionate participant, and as we read his account, much of our fascination comes of our sense of the storyteller being involved. A passage such as that describing the marriage bed is important not so much for its depiction of lust as disgust, but for what it communicates to us of its attraction for the authorial personality. He is repelled by the scene, but he is also fascinated with it. A tremendously dynamic relationship is involved between the author and his story, and when it ends in tragedy, our pity and terror are evoked not only for the protagonist Noemie d'Artiailh, but also and equally as strongly because we sense that this is the only and ultimate resolution that the storyteller has achieved. We have witnessed his struggle with himself to reach that conclusion, and also to keep from reaching it, and so powerfully have his divided sympathies been engaged that when we hear his pronounce his ultimate dramatic judgment, the verdict comes with a rending resolution.

To put the matter bluntly, in *A Kiss for the Leper* François Mauriac not only dramatizes a story; he dramatizes himself as its teller.

Another powerful Mauriac novel in which much the same conditions seem to apply is *Genetrix,* in which all the major characters seem lost, damned souls, consumed in their own selfish desire. Félicité Casenave, the jealous, protective mother, would keep her middleaged only son for her own at the expense of his wife's life. The son, Fernand, weak, insipid, breaks away enough in middle age to yield to desire, and he marries; but he soon repents his error, and gives up his wife's affection for his mother's. Nor is the wife any martyred innocent; Mathilde Lachaissaigne deliberately sets her cap for Fernand Casenave in order to further her worldly position, and when she dies of puerperal infection, it is as she plots reconquest. Early in the novel her own brother Jean, rake and ne'er-do-well, disappears, but not before Mauriac has treated us to a delicious wallow in his description of the markings left upon Jean's body from nocturnal love bouts.

Like so many of Mauriac's provincials of the haute bourgeoisie, these people all seem bereft of spiritual qualities as they seize upon the ownership of humans and things to still the wild emptiness and the rank sensuality of the earth outdoors—the winds, the pines of the Landes, the sounds, the smells, the terrain. Old Numa Casenave, proprietor of the estate, sleeps in his grave which he ordered covered with the clay he owned. Beyond the windows the locomotives rush past, whistles shrieking in the Bordeaux night. There is no Grace for those who people this novel.

When his wife dies, Fernand Casenave blames his mother, though he too is guilty. Only then does he realize how old Félicité has kept him from life. Eventually Félicité too dies, of a stroke that comes when Fernand tells her that he will be good to her again, but because the dead wife would have desired him to be. Only the widowed son is left now, stunned and almost helpless, while the servants take advantage of the situation to install themselves in the house. Then in a sudden reversion to his dead mother's iron will and harshness, Fernand drives out the usurping serpents. In death Félicité has triumphed. In the end Fernand is living out his sullen, solitary existence in the gloomy old house, and only the old servant Marie de Lados, whose children had attempted to take over, comes back at the close to touch his forehead, wait upon his needs.

It is not difficult to see why much of the most harsh criticism made of Mauriac has been by Catholics, who are quick to note the compulsive psychological relationship between Mauriac's Jansenist wrath against the treachery of the flesh and his lurid fascination with the fleshly processes. How can the body as described by Mauriac be the Temple of the Holy Ghost? And it is also true that the very zeal with which Mauriac goes about detailing the horrors of the life of carnal sin has the effect not only of building up considerable sympathy for the unfortunate mortals so addicted (Mauriac would not object to this), but indeed of suggesting the attractiveness of the sinful life! Given the nature of Mauriac's artistry, this is not surprising. In his best novels there is a tortured dialectic between body and soul, and though the outcome of this struggle is inevitable, the progress toward the conclusion has many fascinating artistic and psychological bypaths. The literary artist in Mauriac, it should be emphasized, surely arises in large part *out of the opposition between* the Jansenist and the sensualist. The result is that there is much that is fascinating and murkily attractive about Mauriac's appalled view of the sensual life. No wonder Catholic critics have been concerned with the seductive power of sin when denounced by François Mauriac!

But if one considers the terrible outcome of almost all of Mauriac's sinners, the shriveling of their human attributes, there is additional ground for theological objection to Mauriac. Rayner Heppenstall, who is not a Catholic, sums up the case against

Mauriac in *The Double Image,* a study of "mutations of Christian mythology" in four Catholic French writers. His points are chiefly two.

First,

The Jansenist gloom is oppressive. The peasants are too abject, their masters too greedy and self-righteous, the young people much too far along the primrose path to the everlasting bonfire. The vale of tears through which M. François Mauriac drags his characters is unrelieved. Nobody sings. Nobody dances. Nobody is good-looking, except as a sign of degeneracy. Copulation is a long-drawn, serpertine agony. Nobody has any fun at all.

Secondly,

The trend of Mauriac's religous apologetic is so to present the world that without God it would be intolerable. The existence of God is therefore proved in the sense that it is shown to be pragmatically necessary. This is the most desperate atheism. Or perhaps it should be regarded simply as magic and conjuration. By creating an artificial vacuum, Mauriac would appear to lay compulsion upon the uncreated to produce some entity capable of filling it.[19]

Once again one is reminded of Mauriac's beloved Pascal, with his famed wager on the existence of God—that if God in truth exists, one will only lose by betting that He doesn't, while if there is no God, nothing can be lost by acting as if there were one. To prove God's existence by the depiction of a world intolerable without Him is indeed a most negative way of approaching divinity. It is as if Dante had chosen to end the *Comedy* with the poet's precarious descent from Hell.

Yet which of the three books of the *Divine Comedy* has made the greatest dramatic impression upon its readers? By all odds the answer is the *Inferno,* and in it one especially senses the

19. Heppenstall, p. 62.

poet's own passionate involvement in what he has created. Here the case for François Mauriac as novelist rests—both theologically, I think, and artistically. The artist in Mauriac, as I have said before, surely is the product of the human dialectic between this world and the next, which marks his best fiction. No wonder, then, that in Mauriac's better novels, few characters ever possess the Grace that is the hope of Mauriac's Jansenist Catholicism. The work of art, to repeat, must embrace appearances, and though its meaning may be Revealed Truth, it cannot itself *be* that Truth. In Mauriac's instance, the struggle to divest oneself of the things of this world is dramatized. This in itself is inevitably a negative process. Anything else would be not Image but Truth. It would not be fiction at all.

Precisely here, I think, one finds not only the answer to Sartre's objection that Mauriac "intrudes" into his narrative instead of rendering it objectively from without, but an insight into one kind of formal relationship between literature and religion. To get at this, I want to take up another of Mauriac's major novels, *Thérèse Desqueyroux* (published in this country by Doubleday Anchor Books, along with several short stories and the novel entitled *The End of the Night*, as *Thérèse*).

The heroine of this novel is a young woman who has attempted to poison her husband. The story is related through flashbacks, and it opens as Thérèse is freed of the charges against her, thanks to a family cover-up, and begins a railroad journey back to her home in rural Gascony. All during the trip she thinks what she will tell her husband. An intellectual rebel against the smug, property-minded, family-dominated life of the landed bourgeoisie of Mauriac's native Bordeaux country, she had nevertheless married Bertrand Desqueyroux, a typical representative of that life, primarily because she lost her nerve, and was too sympathetic to the cult of property to break loose from all that she knew. Repelled by the physical grossness of her husband's sexual appetite ("He always looked so much in a hurry, so busy, so serious. He was a man of method. 'Do you think it's altogether wise? Thérèse would sometimes ask, appalled by the extent of his virility. . . ." "I always saw Bernard as a man who charged head down at pleasure, while I lay like a corpse, motionless. . . ." [20]), she had nevertheless taken satisfaction in becoming a part of the family establishment after marriage, even to the extent of working in the family's interest (and out of the jealous envy she feels as well) to break up a romance between her husband's young half-sister and a consumptive young man of Portuguese Jewish descent, Jean Azévédo.

She had accomplished this quite handily, but in the process she had fallen in love with Azévédo herself. An intellectual of highly poetic sensibilities, he made Thérèse fully conscious of the extent to which she was now trapped in the suffocating confines of provincial life, with the result that she had sought to kill her husband and thus free herself. Upon her return to her husband following the trial, which constitutes the midway point in the novel, Thérèse finds that Bernard has no intention of taking her back, but instead will force her to live in the same house with him, even go to Mass, in order to maintain the outward show of respectability. At one point she almost takes her own life during this captivity; only the death of an old aunt at the moment she was ready to do so prevents her. Eventually, appearances having been maintained for a sufficiently long period of time to quiet misgivings about the verdict of the trial, the Desqueyroux family is willing to let her go free, and Bernard

20. *Thérèse*, p. 35.

takes her to Paris where he leaves her to her own destiny. From a frustrated, trapped wife in the provinces, she is now a homeless woman in the metropolis, free to pursue her appetites and wishes, but belonging to nobody and to no place. Nothing lies ahead for her except age, boredom, death.

So brief a plot summary gives the impression of a more melodramatic novel than *Thérèse Desqueyroux* is. From the beginning to end, however, the plot is controlled by the style, intense, insistent, sensuous, which makes the story into a compelling psychological portrait of a trapped and desperate woman. Mauriac's relentless uncovering of the mind and heart of Thérèse propels the narrative inexorably forward toward its conclusion, when she is at last "free." But free of what? Imprisoned in the heavy, sullen regimen of provincial life, physically bound to an unimaginative husband for whom her body is only an instrument for sensual gratification, deprived of all emotional outlet and intellectual expression, she took the desperate expedient of violence, only to fail. She was an "outsider"; she did not belong; and her attempt at murder only served to confirm her ultimate captivity. Yet when she is at last turned loose, she has nothing to take its place. From the bondage of provincial boredom she has moved only to a renewed bondage of aimless, rootless desolation.

The theme of the person of sensitivity and spirit trapped in the provincial morass is a frequent one in Mauriac's novels. Mauriac is no physiocrat; he sees nothing ennobling or virtuous in life on the land. For him, daily existence in the Bordeaux in which he grew up and in its surrounding Gascony countryside is brutal and dead. Those who do find it sufficient are themselves spiritually dead, existing without imagination or thought, on a level of biological and material survival, and they can live on the land because they are untroubled by knowledge or intelligence. All they have is appetite and cunning. "The peace and calm of habitual things" which are enough for Bernard Desqueyroux's existence are the sheer blind earth and the flare and freeze of the seasons; they suffice because the sensibility they are able to nourish is not much more than that of an animal.

To Thérèse, life on such terms is maddening, stifling. It affords no expression for the deepest concerns of her spirit, it numbs her senses with heaviness and oppressive sensory rankness. This death-in-life, so suffocating to anyone with sensibilities beyond the brutal level of ordinary provincial existence, impels her toward the most desperate of remedies in order to effect her escape. In order to live, she must commit murder. It is a situation, one notes, very much like that of Emma Bovary, for whom adultery seemed the only escape.

Thérèse's attempted solution fails, but—and here is an important difference between Mauriac the Catholic believer and Flaubert the naturalist—paradoxically it does result in what she thought she desired, her "freedom." Yet this freedom is no solution whatever, for she is not free. She is not, because what she desired—emotional fulfillment, love, the passionate life of the heart—is no more available in Paris than in Argelouse. Jean Azévédo was only the symbol of this life; now that she is in Paris he will no longer want her, for she was for him only a provincial diversion, and when eventually she seeks him out, as she knows she will do, no fulfillment is in store for her.

Thérèse's trap, then, is not the smothering society of the provinces. It is that of being a human, cursed as it were with the instinct for nobler things than land, money, social position, animal gratification. And if Mauriac's sympathy is with her and all such persons, if he values the refusal to subsist on the level of unthinking appetite, he sees her plight as all the more tragic thereby. ("All your light can only reach the knowledge that not in yourselves will you find truth or good," Pascal's dictum goes.) But escaping from the immediate prison of her environment, Thérèse only becomes aware of the larger prison of her human condition.

Thérèse Desqueyroux, then, functions as a religious novel in the negative sense that it depicts, from the Jansenist point of view of its author, the plight of human life without the Grace of God. From Mauriac's theological position, the only thing that might rescue Thérèse is lacking, and that is God's Grace, which takes the form of the human being's eagerness to learn Truth. Without this eagerness, Thérèse can hope for nothing but emptiness.

But—and this is an important clue, I think, to the psychology of a novelist such as Mauriac—the author was *not* willing to abandon Thérèse to her plight. In 1935, a decade later, he took up her case once more, and in *The End of the Night* brought her, through renewed suffering and ordeal, to a state in which "pardon and the peace of God" were at last possible to her. Judged artistically the sequel is much less successful than its predecessor, but this is not my concern here. The point is that however much Mauriac the theologian may have loathed the human condition he described in *Thérèse Desqueyroux*, Mauriac the human being could not acquiesce in so dismal a verdict. There is no reason to suppose that this ambivalence about the meaning of the life of Thérèse was not equally present, if not yet overtly evident, when Mauriac wrote his first novel about her. Though Mauriac's theology may have instructed him that the struggle of a Thérèse is useless, that "the filth of flesh" is unimportant and must be sublimed away, the human insight and compassion that make Mauriac a great novelist ennobled Thérèse Desqueyroux's character to the point where her human condition was *not* worthless, *not* meaningless. Thus this religious novel, which is to say this novel in which the meaning is designed to justify God's Truth, becomes indeed a drama of salvation, and this in large part because we can observe that drama taking place not only in what happens to the fictional characters. but from the standpoint of an author who is of two minds about the whole thing.

This, once again, is what I mean about a formal relationship existing between author and story. In such a novel as Mauriac's, the author is constantly making us aware of his authorial presence as he works out the divided loyalties inside himself through what he tells us about what is going on. He establishes for us a position from which to observe the events of the novel. But this position is no mere technique involving the point of view. It involves as well a moral dilemma, which we are made to sense. On the one hand, Mauriac keeps reminding us how filthy is the flesh, how rank and distasteful the human condition, how futile the effort to escape from it, how terrible the wretched plight of the human being. On the other hand, he keeps trying to explain to us *why* Thérèse had to do what she did, why she is a worthy human being, why she seeks passion and love, why she should have our sympathy and our own identification with her plight. Back and forth this ambivalence, this argument operates, compelling us to look this way and that, share this perspective and that as we follow Thérèse's story. We become not only an observer of the action, not only privy to the thoughts of the protagonist, but also and at the same time deeply involved with the moral perspective of the authorial personality by whom the action and characterization are being revealed.

Mauriac accomplishes this business of drawing us into his perspective in part by structural devices. He prefaces his novel, for example, with a statement about his own relationship to Thérèse, explains why as a novelist he chose to "give imagined life" to

her. Our consciousness of the novelist's presence is heightened
by the immediate establishment of a viewpoint for observation
which, while it encompasses Thérèse's thought's, stands off from
her and describes her as she thinks and acts. She hears a conversation between her father and her lawyer only with difficulty;
for us it is made quite plain. Mauriac comments on the season
of the year, though Thérèse is not thinking about it. We listen
with her, are told what she is thinking. Then, as she prepares
to get into the cab and as she thinks about her father, Mauriac
informs us of what the father is thinking at that moment.
Thérèse converses with the lawyer and with her father, tells the
lawyer she will soon be returning to live with her father. Non-
sense, the father replies, you must live with your husband from
now on. She agrees with him. The father wonders to himself
why she could have said what she did. The lawyer thinks about
how, if the trial had not ended successfully but had gone on to
a higher court, another advocate would have taken over in his
place. With that the first section of the novel concludes.

Obviously we are not only watching *with* Thérèse; like the
watchbird, we are also *watching* Thérèse. And as the story continues we are drawn further into this authorial perspective, and
made to share its moral ambivalence. And the authorial personality never deserts us; repeatedly he tells us things that
Thérèse herself doesn't know. Each time it is for the purpose of
instructing us how to view what is happening.

Yet the structural machinery is only part of Mauriac's
method of bringing us into participation with his moral perspective. More importantly, we are also made to take part in
the struggle going on within Mauriac as he decides about
Thérèse and others. He does not adopt a consistent attitude
toward Thérèse, as one might do were one preaching a sermon
with Thérèse as exemplar. Instead his attitude shifts; at one

point he is favorable to her life and hopes, at another he judges them coldly and ruthlessly, from the standpoint both of their moral worth and of their pragmatic effectiveness. We are made, by the way the novelist tells his story, to look at Thérèse's thoughts and behavior along with him, from several points of view. And the working out of all this, as the novel moves towards a climax, creates a mounting tension, between human and theological points of view, which we are made to share, until at the last, when the story is done, we both share Thérèse's plight and view it from the standpoint of its moral inevitability, to the end that it seems both unavoidable and regrettable, morally just and humanly pathetic. The result is tragedy, and in fairly strict Aristotelian terms at that.

This particular moral position, this resolution in the form of a final awareness of the meaning of what has taken place, characterizes the religious novel as practiced by François Mauriac. The religious position has been dramatized in terms of the authorial personality creating it. Such dramatization would have been impossible had Mauriac been able or willing to tell the story entirely from the standpoint of his Jansenist belief. All that would have resulted in would have been a parable. From the standpoint of religious Truth, there would have been no excuse for the human sympathy with appearances that constitutes Thérèse's part of the argument. But instead Mauriac the artist, the human sinner, the sensualist, got equally involved in the dialectic along with Mauriac the religious apologist, and the result was not a sermon but a novel, one of the finest religious novels ever written.

I have concentrated my attention on a few of Mauriac's best novels, to the exclusion of most of the others. I should have liked to discuss at some length *The Desert of Love*, a work that many critics think among Mauriac's finest. Instead only a brief comment is appropriate. The novel chronicles the bondage of a middleaged Bordeaux physician and his adolescent son to a woman named Maria Cross. The lady's name is obviously both ironic and pathetic, in that in her sensual appeal and her feminine mystery she stands for the human image that human beings must pursue when God's Grace embodied in the reality of the Virgin is lacking. Mauriac's depiction of the respectable, dignified old medical man helplessly desiring the younger, kept woman is movingly drawn; the doctor is willing to sacrifice career and reputation if need be, but the affair never goes that far. Equally convincing is Mauriac's handling of the appeal of the same woman to the mixed spiritual and physical desires of the doctor's son. But the novel, I feel, is less than a total success because of what I consider its implausibility. One accepts the passion of both father and son for Maria, but not what Mauriac insists that it *does* to the young man. Tempted by Maria and then rejected when he seeks to make love to her, the young man abandons himself to seventeen years of profligacy. The novel is centered on his encounter with Maria in a Paris night club, and his memories of what she had been to him, and what she has done to him. This may be possible, but seventeen years would seem a long time for a young man— even one of François Mauriac's young men—to suffer over a rejection.

The difficulty, I suspect, comes in a clash between what Mauriac wanted Maria Cross to symbolize—the desert of human love unwatered by God—and what the demands of characterization and fictional plausibity would dictate. The result, I fear, is melodrama; though it is only fair to point out that for so astute a critic as Turnell, *The Desert of Love* is an entire success,

a remarkable presentation of a predicament which is becoming increasingly the predicament of modern man . . . who is caught in the spiritual-emotional wilderness through the atrophy of his religious sense and who is faced with the choice between a living death and a sudden violent end—or the miracle which on this occasion at least the novelist fortunately does not try to provide.[21]

Perhaps this is true, but I nevertheless find it difficult to believe fully in that seventeen-year debauch of young Raymond Courréges all because Maria Cross did him wrong.

Earlier I noted my disagreement with Turnell's assertion that in *Viper's Tangle* Mauriac's doctrinal concerns intrude so forcibly on his fiction that the characterization fails. It is true, however, that after that novel this is what happens to Mauriac. *The Frontenacs* follows *Viper's Tangle* by one year in the Mauriac canon, and while the book is by no means a disaster, it is definitely a step down from the high drama of Mauriac's major work. Philip Stratford declares that Mauriac intended *The Frontenacs* "as an antidote to the previous novel." He set out to celebrate family life and family solidarity "in an attempt to counterbalance that one-sided picture of avarice and self-interest" that is *Viper's Tangle*.[22] If so, this autobiographical picture of a provincial family, with its gentle evocation of the Bordeaux countryside, fails to balance the scales. The story of three brothers, a widow, and an uncle, it is pleasant enough, but only in one scene, that in which the older brother clashes with his wife about whether his mother is to come and live with them, does one glimpse the intensity and drama with which Mauriac can illuminate a human situation. The truth seems to be— and one is reminded of both Hemingway's and Faulkner's later work and its relationship to their major novels—that when Mauriac abandons for the moment his announced goal of depicting the Catholic universe of evil, and attempts to write

21. *The Art of French Fiction*, p. 329.
22. *Faith and Fiction: Creative Process in Greene and Mauriac*, p. 244.

about decent, God-fearing folk, there is a marked falling-off in fictional intensity.

Why is this? I fear that the reason is tightly bound up in the psychology of the author. One recalls Mr. Leo Durocher's remark, in another field of artistic endeavor, that "nice guys finish last." Whatever the cause, it seems inescapable that Mauriac's major novels all involve that characteristic dialectic between flesh and spirit, with the authorial personality's sensibilities as Jansenist and as suffering human deeply engaged, and that when this tension between two worlds is removed, all of Mauriac's skill with language and description, all of the tenderness with which he invests the scenes of his provincial childhood, cannot make up for its absence.

The best of Mauriac's later work is said to be *Woman of the Pharisees* (1946). The novel centers on the activities of one Brigitte Pian, a hardhearted, puritanical woman who considers herself one of the Lord's Anointed. Having caused her daughter great pain and frustration, having succeeded in getting a kindly and understanding abbé dismissed from his curacy, and having caused the death of a young woman who married in opposition to her will, Brigitte ultimately realizes her own hypocrisy, is overcome with remorse, and in sorrow and humiliation for her sins she awaits God's Grace. But the difficulty, it seems to me, is that Mauriac the Jansenist who believes in the redemptive power of Grace, and Mauriac the human being who is horrified by the sanctimonious cruelty of this domineering woman, fail to become involved in the expected dialectic. When Mauriac wrote about sinners trying in vain to achieve love and fulfillment through the flesh, he was able imaginatively to take the part of the suffering sinners, and this produced an authorial personality with the necessary psychological opposition to the Jansenism. But in *Woman of the Pharisees* no such thing happens. For most of the novel he is intent upon showing the vicious-ness of his religious hypocrite, and when he turns around and begins to show her becoming remorseful and humble, he is forced to try to graft onto the earlier characterization a muta-tion which, however much it may accord with the theology of Grace, is fictionally so unprepared and so unconvincing that it seems manipulated for doctrinal purposes.

In *Viper's Tangle*, which has a similar problem of characteri-zation, a transformation was possible because Mauriac's dialectic of body and soul had been preparing the reader for what was to happen, however much one did not realize it at the time. In *Woman of the Pharisees* there has not been such preparation, and the change seems unbelievable when it occurs.

At this point an interesting question arises. If, as I have sought to show, the dramatic tension of a Mauriac novel involves not only the struggle of the protagonists, but the developing division of loyalties within the authorial personality telling the story, then why indeed should a novel such as *Woman of the Pharisees* fail? Is there not still very much the sense of a struggle on the storyteller's part to make his novel mean what he thinks it ought to mean? Indeed, is not his very failure to make the meaning come across with dramatic conviction, so far as the characterization is concerned, a highly interesting business in its own right?

The answer, I think, is that while this authorial struggle may indeed be interesting from a biographical standpoint, it is not artistically, which is to say imaginatively, made a part of the novel. When in *Thérèse Desqueyroux* we sense the author agon-izing over what he knows will have to be Thérèse's degradation, and we perceive the tangled complexity of his attitude toward Thérèse and her story, it is his close and continual emotional involvement in the situation that attracts us, that interests us in him as well as the story he is telling. But in a novel such as *Woman of the Pharisees*, there is no such involvement on his part. His decision to save Brigitte Pian from Hell is intellectual, not emotional, because he has never really gotten his own personality into the drama at all. The so-called authorial personality, the implied author, never becomes fictionally alive for us, which is to say, he never gets into his story. His role is no longer that of novelist; it is that of theologian, who dispenses Truth from on high and from outside the novel. Here Sartre is right; Mauriac *is* to that extent playing God, and what we perceive is the sight of the author doing just that. The relationship between this author and his story is not dramatic; it is ideological, and the art of fiction has nothing to do with what is going on.

Sartre is correct, then, when he maintains that the novelist must deal with Appearances rather than with Truth. But no doubt his dictum is equally applicable not merely to so-called religious novels, but to "Marxist" novels, "naturalistic" novels —any kind of novel, that is, in which the author is writing out of a preconceived ideological structure which prescribes *ex cathedra* what the meaning of human experience is to be. From the standpoint of fiction as Appearance, therefore, it ought not to be possible to write a genuinely religious novel, or a genuinely Marxist or naturalistic or any other kind of novel governed and structured by a revealed truth; as the old argument puts it, true Christian tragedy is by definition an impossibility.

But in Mauriac's instance we have seen what happens. In his better work, the novelist, instead of acting as God, interposes his authorial personality as a kind of intermediary between Truth and Appearance. In his attempt to set forth the human consequences of religious Truth, he fights out the meaning with himself, and the struggle to square his human sympathies with his religious convictions projects itself into the way he tells his story; he is engaged emotionally in the story he is writing, and the sense of his engagement makes available a keenly dramatic excitement to the reader. Not for nothing does Dante make himself swoon upon being confronted with the situation of Paolo and Francesca.

Our authorial personality, then, must not only be present, but he must be involved. He must care what is going on in his story, and that implies, from the reader's standpoint, the sense of the author's having a strong emotional stake in the story he is telling. For through emotions, not through ideas, are fictional characters created, and if the authorial personality who tells us a story exists in a formal relationship to the story, then he would appear to have to exist for us as a fictional creation, and be bound by the same laws that make all fictional characters successful: they must be human and believable, they must feel as well as think, and their ideas must be part of their humanity, must be *believed* as well as thought.

All of which leads, by a very long route that has involved an examination of the work of six novelists, to the point I have sought to make in this book: the author of a novel is a character in his fiction, and part of his art is that of dramatizing himself.

EIGHT · Postscript: The Essential Author

1. Call me Ishmael. Some years ago—never mind how long precisely—having little or no money in my purse, and nothing particular to interest me on shore, I thought I would sail about a little and see the watery part of the world. It is a way I have of driving off the spleen, and regulating the circulation. . . .[1]

2. When Caroline Meeber boarded the afternoon train for Chicago, her total outfit consisted of a small trunk, a cheap imitation alligator-skin satchel, a small lunch in a paper box, and a yellow leather snap purse, containing her ticket, a scrap of paper with her sister's address in Van Buren Street, and four dollars in money. It was in August, 1889. She was eighteen years of age, bright, timid, and full of the illusions of ignorance and youth. . . .[2]

3. From a little after two o'clock until almost sundown of the long still hot weary dead September afternoon they sat in what Miss Coldfield still called the office because her father had called it that—a dim hot airless room with the blinds all closed and fastened for forty-three summers because when she was a girl someone had believed that light and moving air carried heat and that dark was always cooler, and which (as the sun shone fuller and fuller on that side of the house) became latticed with yellow slashes full of dust motes which Quentin thought of as being flecks of the dead old dried paint itself blown inward from the scaling blinds as wind might have blown them. . . .[3]

1. Herman Melville, *Moby-Dick*, Signet Classics ed. (New York, 1961), p. 21.
2. Theodore Dreiser, *Sister Carrie*, Laurel ed. (New York, 1960), p. 23.
3. William Faulkner, *Absalom, Absalom!* (New York, 1936), p. 7.

What kind of game is it that we play when we pretend that either of those three openings of distinguished American novels is "impersonal," the writing of an anonymous, effaced author who was content to let his story speak for itself and who never tried to introduce himself into his narrative?

1. Melville is not Ishmael? Of course Melville never roomed with Queequeg at the Spouter Inn, or floated alone atop a coffin in the South Pacific after all his whaling shipmates had gone down with the *Pequod*. But Ishmael *is* Melville all the same— so is Ahab, for that matter—and we know it. We know it because Ishmael and Ahab can tell us what things mean, and can stand away from the narrative and address themselves to us. Ishmael plays a double role; he takes part in the story, and from outside the scope of the plot he tells us what is important about it and what it means. When he tells us what the events mean, he expresses judgments, and through these he shows us what manner of fellow he is. When a fictional narrator or character becomes the repository of Truth, when what he thinks and says to us is intended not to relate an aspect of the dramatic situation to himself as character, but to tell the reader what he ought to think about the situation, he ceases to that extent to be a character alone and becomes the author's surrogate as well. The author in turn is thereby involved in a fictional role; he becomes a distinct personality whose presence implies certain attitudes toward and evaluations of what is going on. Woe betide him if ever we catch him falsifying the record by insisting on meanings and judgments that are not justified by the story he has told us! When Thomas Wolfe insists that Eugene Gant's whole life has been forever blighted and the joy has gone out of the world to return no more because Eugene's play has been turned down by a producer, it is not Eugene Gant we smile at; it is Thomas Wolfe.

2. Theodore Dreiser never appears in *Sister Carrie* as a narrator; but it is Dreiser who informs us that Carrie's satchel is cheap and imitation, that she is "bright, timid, and full of the illusions of ignorance and youth." If one examines the way critics have written about Dreiser's novels, any doubts of Dreiser's presence as authorial personality should vanish. There is constant reference to his "brooding pity" and his "profound sense of wonder." What Dreiser does in *Sister Carrie,* for example, is to set out to describe Carrie's rise to power and the varying fortunes of those she uses along the way. The rise of Carrie is perfectly in accordance with Dreiser's notion of naturalism, the survival of the fit, and so forth. But Dreiser does not merely show us this; he tells it to us, commenting on it all the while, making his points, and continually shaking his head and muttering, "Isn't it terrible, simply terrible, the way life has got to be?" It has often been remarked that it is puzzling just why Dreiser's novels are so moving, when he wrote the English language so poorly. But what Dreiser did was to dramatize himself, and never more so than in those clumsy, purple poetic passages of lament. Remove these passages and something essential is missing from *Sister Carrie:* the blundering characterization of the author telling a sad and moving story, and not quite able to articulate why the story moves him so. The integrity of such passages is guaranteed by what the author has told us about Carrie and her life; their very crudeness seems appropriate.

3. With Faulkner we are from the start in the hands of a master storyteller who goes to great pains to make sure that we look at what happens in his novels in the proper way. There can be no question that the description of Rosa Coldfield's house in the first paragraph of *Absalom, Absalom!* is given to us coldly and objectively; it is heavily suffused in an observer's mood and

attitude. Much of the dispute over who "tells" the Faulkner novels can be settled if we understand the way Faulkner sets up his authorial consciousness as the center of the novel's meaning. In *As I Lay Dying,* for example, how can Addie Bundren, who is dead, "think" several monologues as the Bundrens prepare to take her body to town for burial? Because the center of consciousness, the focal point on which everything in that novel depends, is concerned with her as thinking what she does. The existence of that authorial consciousness is implied in every one of the numerous monologues by Bundrens and others that constitute the developing story. In *The Sound and the Fury* the idiot Benjy doesn't know the words for what he thinks; the authorial voice supplies them. In this novel, the novelist becomes the focal point and interpreter of what everybody is thinking. And we, in the role of his congregation, trust him to tell us what we need to know.

How can Faulkner do this? How can he assume that we will believe what he says an idiot is thinking? How can he be so sure that we will not boggle at clairvoyance or violation of "point of view" when we read *As I Lay Dying?* Because he knows that we have as readers entered into a compact with him upon beginning his book. The compact, which is nothing more or less than a convention, is that we will let him tell us the story his way, and not hold him to ordinary conditions of "real-life" reportage, in return for being shown something about human experience that will make the agreement worth our while.

Every novel that has ever existed is the product of this compact. In the first chapter I noted that one of its provisions is that a story is being told, and real life is not being experienced. The slightest suspicion that this particular provision is being violated is enough to imperil the novel for the reader. The role

of the authorial personality is something that must be strictly
observed; if we get the impression that the author is seeking
to discuss aspects of his own life which are not proper to his
role as authorial personality, we draw back uneasily. When
the narrator of *Remembrance of Things Past* begins turning
Saint Loup and other unlikely candidates into homosexuals, we
get a hint of compulsive behavior, and instead of the novel
remaining a magnificent search for lost time, we think to ourselves that the biographical Marcel Proust seems to be trying
to make us condone homosexuality by turning his most masculine characters into homosexuals. The shock of this sudden abuse
of the authorial status for purposes other than telling the story
threatens to imperil the story—until Proust drops it and we
are again caught up in his story for its own sake. On the other
hand, we will accept personal reference after personal reference
on Stendhal's part, because he uses such things to bolster and
enhance his role as authorial personality, and not vice versa.
Thus anything in real life can be used in a novel, but its logic
must always be based on its relationship to the authorial personality telling the story. It is not that Proust needs to justify
homosexuality; we will accept homosexuality in a novel. It is
that as authorial personality, this is not the position the narrator had been taking; and not only that, but many of the narrator's most moving insights have been made possible because
he has taken another position—he has, for example, made us
laugh at the way the Baron de Charlus suspects everyone of
being a potential homosexual. To have the author next begin
doing it himself is profoundly disturbing. In another novel it
might have been quite acceptable. The logic, to repeat, is
whether it works with the particular novel, the particular author telling us his story.

The authorial personality's role, in other words, must be

consistent, just as the role of any fictional character must be consistent. Whether it is true to the biographical, real-life role of the novelist is irrelevant. It is difficult for anyone thus to "lie" in print and get away with it, but by no means impossible. When Proust writes *The Cities of the Plain* as if he were not a homosexual, he largely gets away with it. When Dreiser tries to write about the social life of the idle rich, in *An American Tragedy,* the episodes involved reek of falseness—because much of the triumph of Dreiser's art is based on the envy and longing with which he can look at material wealth and social polish from the outside. The test in each case, to repeat, is not authorial biography, but authorial *authority.* We must believe in the personality telling the story.

Proust, in his attack on the method of Sainte-Beuve, insists that the real author is to be found in his work, not in the accidents of his life. "A book," Proust says, "is the product of a different *self* from the self we manifest in our habits, in our social life, in our vices." If we recall that the form of the *Contre Sainte-Beuve* is that of a dialogue with his mother, we might speculate a little as to why Marcel Proust might have thought it important to insist on that point. But the biographical inquiry thus suggested does not invalidate the point Proust makes, which is a sound observation; Proust knew that the reason we pay so much attention to Stendhal is that Stendhal exists, not that there once was a man named Beyle, and therefore that the way to find out who he was is through his performance as Stendhal, and not through Beyle.

We are suspicious, and with reason, of such biographical criticism as Sainte-Beuve exemplified; only during the past several decades have we overthrown the dead, inert domination of an historical scholarship that concerned itself with authors and with subject matter instead of with poems and stories. It has been a long battle to convince Professor Dryasdust that what Ishmael makes of the doubloon that Captain Ahab nails to the masthead is of much greater relevance and importance than an historical inquiry into Spanish coinage, plus conjectures as to where and when Herman Melville may have seen this or that coin.

In order to win that battle, however, we have had to over-simplify the proper division between created artistic work and the history of the creator. We have insisted that the personality of the author is not important to the way in which we read his novel. The fact is, however, that the actual division is not between an author and an objective, dramatized work of art; it is between an author as storyteller and the author as bio-graphical figure. For the author as storyteller—the authorial personality revealed in the novel—is very much a part of our experience in reading his novel. To pretend that he is not present is an error. We should instead insist that the author we are concerned with when we read or write about a novel is the author there before us in the novel, and not some carrion corpse long since dead and buried.

Beyle may be dead; Stendhal is very much alive. Much of my enjoyment of *The Red and the Black* and *The Charterhouse of Parma* stems from the pleasure of his company. However im-perfectly I may have grasped, or failed to grasp, what his presence means and how it manifests itself, however inconsistent and pedestrian these inquiries into certain great novelists and novels may be, that presence, and nothing more or less, is what I have tried to describe in this book.

Index

218